World University Library

The World University Library is an international series
of books, each of which has been specially commissioned.
The authors are leading scientists and scholars from all over
the world who, in an age of increasing specialization, see the
need for a broad, up-to-date presentation of their subject.
The aim is to provide authoritative introductory books for
students which will be of interest also to the general
reader. Publication of the series takes place in Britain,
France, Germany, Holland, Italy, Spain, Sweden and
the United States.

Karl Otmar von Aretin

The Papacy and
the Modern World

Translated by Roland Hill

World University Library

**McGraw-Hill Book Company
New York Toronto**

Acknowledgments

Acknowledgment is due to the following for the illustrations (the number refers to the page on which the illustration appears): 17 Giraudon, Paris; 18 Bulloz, Paris; 46, 100, 103, 109 Mansell Collection; 53 Musée de Versailles; 68 Museo di Roma; 73, 99, 154 Mr James Langdale; 85 Istituto per la Storia del Risorgimento Italiano; 98 National Portrait Gallery, London; 106 Universal Photo-Service; 123 Miss Marguerite Steen; 183, 195, 219, 231 Pontificia Fotografia; 184, 208 Institute of Contemporary History; 207 Keystone Press Agency; 211 Internat. Bilder-Agentur, Zurich.

The map on page 81 is based on one in *The Recent History Atlas*, Martin Gilbert (cartography by John Flower). The maps on pages 168-9 and 228-9 were researched by Anthony Spencer, Pastoral Research Centre. All the maps were drawn by Design Practitioners Ltd.

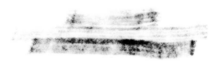

Phototypeset by BAS Printers Limited, Wallop, Hampshire, England
Manufactured by LIBREX, Italy.

Contents

Introduction

Briefly listed, the most important movements in the period of roughly 170 years covered by this book are nationalism, restoration, liberalism, socialism, imperialism, the Russian Revolution, parliamentary democracy and fascism. Most of these had within them a strong Christian element. However, apart from the restoration, the papacy never wholly identified itself with any one of these. Yet equally, it was not able to shirk them, nor the problems that they brought, and indeed it came in direct conflict with the majority of these movements. The emergence of national churches was the problem threatening the spiritual supremacy of the popes in the eighteenth century. In Rome nothing met with such relentlessly thorough opposition as the nineteenth-century national-church tendencies; while to this day liberalism is seen by Rome as the greatest enemy of the Catholic church. Moreover, parliamentary democracy has long been viewed with mistrust and rejected as a product of liberalism. For all Pope Leo XIII's personal interest in the social question, Catholic teaching on social matters, never formulated with complete clarity, has done no more than indicate the right direction. Atheistic socialism, in particular the Russian Revolution, became the church's greatest enemy.

Originally, the converting of non-European peoples was the vital impulse behind the voyages of discovery of the sixteenth and seventeenth centuries. If in the nineteenth century imperialism had long since managed without this element, then in the second half of that century and in the twentieth century Christian missionary work still played an important part within colonial government. The Catholic church, here as elsewhere, put herself all too willingly at the disposal of the liberal state that she shunned in other respects.

From this a discrepancy emerges that is of decisive importance for the relation of the Catholic church to the modern world. A romantic enthusiasm for the Middle Ages as a period which was in some way 'saved' increasingly took from the papacy its means of assessing the present. But because Catholicism as a whole increased in importance during the nineteenth century and did not lose its character as a formative power, the modern world and the Catholic church clashed on a whole series of important questions. In each of these the papacy, if it took a positive and constructive attitude to the world, emerged with the support of public opinion. These clashes thus brought about different effects, which made the papacy, despite its denial of the modern world, into one of its formative influences. The history of papal debates with contemporary society is therefore closely linked to political, social and economic history. However, this history obeys other laws, in as much as the popes were not in this period among the leading influences of their day.

The papacy's denial of the modern world, and in particular of democracy which guaranteed the freedom of the individual, favoured the emergence of fascist regimes in the 1920's. Yet in disputing the totalitarian claim of these dictatorships the Christian churches, and not least Catholicism, showed their importance for the world today. Vatican II confirmed this trend, and thus became the great intellectual event of the mid century. For some time after, the papacy seemed to be at the forefront of the progressive movements. In the Netherlands, France, South America, Germany, Spain and Italy, a new Catholicism began to be felt. Forces which had arisen in the European fight for freedom against Nazi Germany emerged once more.

The events surrounding the encyclical *Humanae vitae* have accentuated the special dilemma of the pope since Vatican II, and in particular have shown that the Council managed to achieve nothing more for Catholicism than the possibility of opening itself to contemporary events and imbuing these with its spirit. The attempt to solve a question bearing on all humanity by an authoritarian papal decision unconvincing in argument and all too much reflecting inherited church attitudes, has revealed the problem of

how far the church should open itself to the world, which was over-
looked in the euphoric atmosphere of Vatican II. The pope lost the
world's attention at the moment when, in a question affecting the
whole world, he addressed himself only to Catholics and consequently reopened the problem unanswered since the Reformation:
is the pope merely the head of the Catholic church and thus responsible for Catholics alone, or is he Christ's representative on
earth and thus speaking to all mankind? The great popes have
always acknowledged their responsibility for the whole world. So
what is in question here goes far beyond the content of *Humanae
vitae*. We see the dilemma of the Roman administrative system of
the *curia*, which in its present form goes back to the second half of
the nineteenth century, and its inability to grasp the problems of
the modern world. That this world was not unreceptive to the
Christian message had been shown by the world-wide response
to the Council and its impulses. For those with an
understanding of history there was nothing new in this. The
conflict outlined in this book between the papacy and the modern
world over some 170 years shows countless examples of this
openess, this responsiveness. During the last century and a half the
popes have avoided such a confrontation whenever it threatened to
go beyond the accepted forms – an attitude which has had grave
consequences for both the papacy and mankind. Vatican II has
proved that there are ways to shape this world anew and belong
with it in the Christian spirit. If the papacy avoids the problems
that this brings, then the Catholic church will soon be reduced to
an insignificant sect, a danger which was present more than once
in the nineteenth century.

Our world today is undergoing an undreamt-of spiritual upheaval. No institution will emerge unchanged from this revolution,
and those who hold inflexibility to be a virtue in contemporary
institutions are liable to find themselves excluded in future from an

active part in answering spiritual questions. Most modern trends in intellectual, economic and political matters date from the nineteenth century and are now seeking new forms. In this sense the papacy differs little from marxism, liberalism, parliamentary democracy and all the other determining factors of our time. But on the other hand its unprecedented chance, in this upheaval, of being among the formative influences must not be ignored. Papacy and modern world thus transcend the confines of an historical problem: their confrontation enshrines some of the great spiritual challenges which our century has to face.

Part 1

Reform Catholicism
and the French
Revolution

There is a deep symbolism in the fact that, at the very moment when the great dream of the Renaissance popes became reality and the dome of St Peter's was completed, Christendom lost its world-embracing universality, or in other words, its catholicity. The Basilica was intended to symbolise the uniting of the rule of St Peter and the ancient rule of Rome, but came instead to represent a papacy of greatly diminished importance. When the plans were first drawn up, the papacy ruled supreme in the ecclesiastical councils; when the building was completed, the popes ruled only over the Spanish and Italian peninsulas and no one knew whether France, Germany and Poland would remain Catholic or succumb to the new Protestantism.

This rift added to the papalism of the old Catholic world and increased the anti-papal tendency, which was an old phenomenon within the church, among the innovators. But despite the schism the 'old' Catholics never surrendered their Catholic claims to represent the church of Christ on earth. The popes acted no differently towards the schism than they had acted in the past. They condemned the innovators as heretics and excluded them from their communion. The innovators turned no less vehemently against the papacy and, as they called her, the Roman church. The unity of Christendom was shattered.

Since the popes had broken off all connection with the heretics, Europe was divided, from the popes' point of view, into three zones. There was the area in which the religious sovereignty of the popes was uncontested. This comprised Italy, Spain and Portugal. There was another area of Catholic-Protestant co-existence, such as France and Germany, and finally there was the Protestant world completely severed from Rome. While papal relations with the wholly Catholic and the wholly Protestant world remained straight-forward, they assumed an ambiguous character in regard to the mixed denominational, intermediary or 'grey' zone, and this was for two reasons. The Catholicism of this area was not only suspect in Roman eyes, but also differed essentially from Spanish and Italian Catholicism. Important measures of the Council of Trent were never carried out in either France or Germany. In Germany the provisions of the concordat concluded with the princes in 1448 retained their validity, as did those of the concordat of 1516 in France. The episcopate in both countries thus possessed constitutional privileges and duties. In France, with the help of the Edict of Nantes (1598) and the Gallican Liberties (1682), a close connection developed between monarchy and church. French Gallicanism was a national church which acknowledged the pope but denied papal infallibility and central authority.

The character of a national church was largely lacking in the church of Germany, but the very different status of the German bishops was due to the fact that they were temporal princes at the same time. Three spiritual electoral princes participated in the election of the emperor. As heads of various territorial units in the empire, the spiritual princes were closely linked with the constitution of the Reich. On their votes depended the Catholic majority in the Imperial Diet. A breve of Alexander vi, issued in 1500 and reaffirmed by Gregory xiii in 1579, fifteen years after the Council of Trent, assigned the church organisation in Germany to the almost exclusive control of the nobility. The Peace of Westphalia settled the co-existence of the confessions by way of a juridical formula. What was Catholic in 1624 remained Catholic, what was Evangelical remained Evangelical. It was understandable that the popes protested against this solution as much as against the Gallican Articles in France, but they were powerless to change it.

Added to this was the decline of the power of Spain. The fact that the pope no longer governed the whole of Christendom might have been tolerated as long as a wholly Catholic power like Spain was dominant in Europe. But the situation changed when, after the Peace of Westphalia, France took on the Spanish inheritance. France was of course a Catholic state, even more so after the revocation of the Edict of Nantes (1685) and the expulsion of the Huguenots, but the Gallican principles, promulgated against papal opposition, deprived the popes of their jurisdiction in France. This new model of a Catholic national church increased in significance as on the one hand France rose to a position of dominance, and on the other Rome declined to the position of a spiritual and cultural backwater in Europe. In the fifteenth and in the first half of the sixteenth century Rome and Italy were still centres of European thought and culture. This pre-eminence was lost in the seventeenth and eighteenth centuries in which the status of the papacy reached an unprecedented low.

This too was not an accidental development. The discoveries of navigators and astronomers towards the end of the sixteenth century had cast doubt on the picture of the world as the bible painted it. This upheaval affected the whole Christian world; it was resisted by orthodox Protestants no less passionately than by the popes. The famous trial of Galileo demonstrated this resistance. By the middle of the seventeenth century it was clear that the biblical data about the course of the stars and the shape of the earth were false. This was the very moment when the Peace of Westphalia brought about a new political order in which Catholics and heretics confronted each other as equal partners. It was the birth of a new world image based on exact observations, inseparably linked with the work of Descartes. The popes clung to the Ptolemaic system right up to 1822; they rejected the scientific findings as such, and became mere outsiders in the intellectual disputes. The centre of intellectual advance shifted to the north of Europe. In the conflicts over the modern state, which first found expression in France, the Catholic reform movement known as Jansenism that had arisen in the Low Countries was to be of special significance.

1 The modern state and the papacy in the Age of Enlightenment

Jansenism

The movement named after the Dutchman, Cornelius Jansen, aimed originally at a reform of the theology set out by the Council of Trent. Its theological system, based principally upon St Augustine, had gone back to the stricter practices of the early church and was opposed to the exuberant, miracle-loving piety of the Baroque Age. In 1640, two years after Jansen's death, his friends published his *Augustinus* which started the theological dispute. The efforts of the Jansenists to obtain for bishops a status equal to that of the pope proved a serious source of disagreement; their hostility towards the religious orders also brought them into conflict with the Jesuits. Jansenism was condemned for the first time in 1642 by Urban VIII, and various condemnations followed in subsequent years up to the bull *Unigenitus* (1713). These enactments were never accepted by many Catholics, who regarded them as false. They expected that they would be revoked by the eighteenth-century popes, especially by Benedict XIV (1740-58), who was the most important pope of the century and was friendly with Voltaire and other eminent men of his time. Under him Rome became a centre of the Italian Jansenists. 'Nowhere in Italy', wrote Enrico Dammig,[1] 'do we find as powerful a Jansenist movement as in Rome'. Seven cardinals, among them Giuseppe Spinelli who was the indisputable leader of the conclave of 1758, openly admitted to Jansenist sympathies. That is why the condemnations failed to check the spread of Jansenism and its influence within the Catholic church. All the Catholic reform efforts of the eighteenth century, such as Josephinism and Febronianism, contain strong Jansenist elements.

Church-state relations played a special role in the history of Jansenism and other reform movements. Jansenism had a certain kinship with the trends towards a modern, rationalist administration. The Jansenists hoped with the help of the state to achieve

The abbey of Port-Royal, centre of French
Jansenism. It was razed to the ground
by Louis XIV after his reconciliation with
Pope Clement XI. Some of the Jansenists
submitted, others fled to Holland, where they
founded an independent church.

theological reforms that would purify the church. The state, for its part, hoped, by means of Reform Catholicism, to solve the problems of taking on the administrative functions hitherto exercised by the church, and of curtailing ecclesiastical properties, which in some countries amounted to sixty per cent of the land. This process was somewhat one-sidedly defined by the term 'secularisation'. The puritan tendencies of the Jansenists were combined with the efforts of the state to reduce the wealth of the church. In some Catholic countries such as France, Austria, Portugal and the Kingdom of Naples, a close alliance was thus formed between episcopate and monarchy that threatened Rome with exclusion from the discussions concerning reform. As things turned out, the hopes of Reform Catholicism were only very partially fulfilled. The modern state readily availed itself of its help: the Reform Catholic, Jansenist spirit spread to seminaries such as Pavia. But these governmental reforms served only marginally to improve pastoral conditions or ecclesiastical administration; they never met the real concern of Reform Catholics, which was the theological renewal of their church. This issue was always played down. In the eyes of the state the Reform church was merely an institution for the training of good and obedient citizens.

The Reform Catholics were forced to recognise not only that their progressive ideas were rejected by Rome, but also that their theological aims were misunderstood by the state or were regarded as superfluous. The Jansenists in France learned early in the eighteenth century that little trust could be placed in the state and its support. Port-Royal was their great intellectual centre, the members of which exerted a strong influence on Gallicanism and for a long time enjoyed the favour of the French kings. It came to a conflict, however, when the Jansenists took the pope's side against Louis XIV over the *régale,* that is, the king's right to draw revenues from vacant bishoprics and abbaccies, and to appoint bishops and abbots. A brief reconciliation with the popes was the result, but when Clement

XI and Louis XIV again made peace, the king had his revenge on the Jansenists. Port-Royal des Champs was destroyed in 1710. Quesnel and Arnauld, the intellectual leaders of French Jansenism, fled to the Low Countries. These church reformers were tolerated by the king only as long as they served to promote the royal influence.

In the conflict surrounding secularisation the Jesuits became the great enemy of innovation. In Rome the Jesuits were rigid advocates of intransigence, especially in the opposition to Jansenism. They were the consistent advocates of papal primacy, a doctrine which the Reform Catholics opposed the more that the papacy reacted against the enlightenment of the times. They reacted violently against the Jesuits' inexorable antagonism towards Jansenism and its ideas of reform. Hostility towards the curia became widespread among the Catholic intelligentsia in Italy, Germany, France, Spain and Portugal. This hostility had many different roots. One important

LA DEROVTE
ET CONFVSION DES
IANSSENISTES

la Religion   le Pape   la Puissance de l'Eglise

LE PAPE
Puis que du S.t Esprit l'Eglise Illuminée
D'vne fausse doctrine accuse les autheurs
Par le puissance enfin q. Dieu no's a donné
Nous Condamnons leurs doctes to'te Tro'tez

LE ROY
Poussé par les Conseils enfin d'un Dieu Zelé
Qui maintient nos Superstans leper d'Simon
Portons pa'cabelles vne Erreur Criminelle
Le bras de la partie à la Religion

LES IANSSENISTES
Ha que demandevns ne mille's Tonna mesle
Il faut à nos Errevrs renoncer à la fin.
Ou ne sembe su party du doct Calumete
Car le n'e avons bien'tien beaucoup de l'odevr

factor was that secularisation, that is, the limitation of church-
owned land with the state replacing the clergy in administrative
functions, was regarded in Rome as an attack on religion. Rome
saw everywhere only hatred and rejection of the church and provoked further repressive measures. In fairness one has to admit that
even an institution intellectually more flexible than the curia might
have had great difficulty in discerning that the process of secularisation did not really strike at the heart of religion. For the expro-
priations and the abolition of old rights were certainly conducted
with all the appearances of antagonism towards the church. The
names of ministers such as Pombal in Portugal and Tanucci in
Naples came to stand for an unholy anti-Catholic spirit which
attempted to subjugate the church to the state.

Jansenism reached the peak of influence within the Catholic

Contemporary cartoon depicting the betrayal
of the Jansenists by Louis XIV. The Jansenists are seen
fleeing to Calvin; a reference to the fact that their enemies
called them Calvinists. They were actually bitter opponents
of Calvinism and held that the Catholic church
was necessary to salvation.

church at the Synod of Pistoia in 1786, and it was not until 1794
that Pius VI, who was against all concessions to Jansenism, was able
to condemn the decisions of that Synod. Henceforth, Jansenist influence declined, though the corruption of its ideas by the French
Revolution was a factor of at least equal importance in this decline.
This was the beginning of the tragedy which characterised the dis-
ruption of Catholic enlightenment. Internal Catholic reform proved
impossible without Rome, for Rome alone was in a position to give
the necessary support to the ideas of reform. No reform movement
had any chance whatever of succeeding against the combined force
of traditional Catholics and pope.

Just as the ideas of the Enlightenment appealed only to very limited
numbers, so also the ideas of the Jansenists and the Reform Catholics,
who are the intellectual ancestors of liberal Catholicism in the nineteenth century and left-wing Catholics today, reached only a very
small group. For a considerable time this lack of numerical strength
was compensated for by the sympathy which these Catholics enjoyed
among the secular reformers. However, as I have pointed out, the
secular reformers too were far from willing to carry out theological
innovations against the wishes of Rome and disclaimed authority to
do so. They merely exploited the theological reform movement, as
Louis XIV had done, in order to subjugate the church, thereby
following the successful example of the Protestant countries.

The Synod of Pistoia, however, revealed also the weakness of
Jansenism, which was that its appeal lay in a logical and not an
emotional approach. It therefore failed to attract large numbers of
adherents. Their disappointment over this failure induced many
adherents of Jansenism in Italy and France at the end of the century
to go over to the Revolution. They were also influenced in this
decision by the complete indifference of the rulers of enlightened
absolutism to matters of theology. Many of the progressive members
of the French clergy became Revolutionists. When the French

Revolution shook the world, four bishops and 149 priests joined the Third Estate on 23 June 1789. The same happened in Italy at the time of the foundation of the Ligurian and Cisalpine Republics, where the clergy's share in the revolutionary movement was disproportionately large. The famous and notorious Civil Constitution of 1790 by the French clergy expressed the general spirit. After the disappointments with Rome and with enlightened absolutism it was widely felt that the ideals of Reform Catholicism could only be realised with the help of the Revolution and in close alliance with the democratic movement.

This alliance, however, proved fatal. If until that time Catholic reform seemed an enlightened current of Catholicism that enjoyed the respect of secular reformers – its influence on Rousseau and also on Voltaire was not insignificant – it now became the first victim of the shocked reactions caused everywhere by the rule of terror in France. Between 1789 and the rise of Napoleon, Europe was overshadowed by the conviction that reform, regardless of its intentions, was bound to favour subversion and was therefore a work of the devil. This situation provided a new opportunity for the papacy. In its struggle against the clerical supporters of the Civil Constitution it was able, with the help of loyal French Catholics, to deal a blow to Reform Catholicism from which it has never recovered. The attempt to secure the clergy's independence from Rome by agreeing to their new status as civil servants developed into a trial of strength with Rome from which the papacy emerged victorious. The moment had arrived when, with the bull *Auctorem fidei* of 1794 rejecting the decrees of Pistoia, Rome could risk a full condemnation of Jansenist and Reform Catholic ideas.

Rousseau and the French Revolution

A new phase in the history of the popes begins with the alliance between Catholic people and papacy that had already been formed many years earlier against the enlightened, puritan rule of the modern state and that had proved its worth in the French Revolution. What to contemporary observers seemed the darkest years of the papacy was actually the beginning of a triumph which no one could have foreseen in the eighteenth century. It is deeply significant that in 1799, the Camaldolese friar Mauro Cappellari published his book, *Il trionfo della Santa Sede,* in which he anticipated the dogma of papal infallibility. We shall meet him again as Gregory XVI.

But it was not merely the hopes of Reform Catholics that foundered in the French Revolution. A situation of fundamental conflict had emerged with effects that they could not have foreseen.

The essential difference between enlightened absolutism and the democratic republic of the French Revolution in their attitude towards the Catholic church was that the former was satisfied with a supremacy from which all theological questions were excluded. In his efforts to degrade the priesthood to the status of moral watchmen, Joseph II was hardly less radical than the supporters of the French Revolution. That a serious clash with Rome was prevented was due to the Emperor's indifference to religion. Joseph II at least gave *carte blanche* to his priest-officials in other matters, but the French Revolution demanded an identity of state and religion which was intended to integrate the priest-officials into the state as much as into the church. A government which was indifferent although not hostile to religion could accommodate itself to the church, but attempts by the state to unify state and church, though with full recognition of the religious aspect of Catholicism, led to the most serious conflicts. The church's integration into and subjection to the state, achieved in the name of enlightened absolutism, was brought

Frontispiece of the 1832 edition of
Il Trionfo della Santa Sede, a work
in which Gregory XVI, as a simple
Camaldolese monk, had in 1799 predicted
the victory of the Holy See over national
(especially the Gallican) churches.

about without great difficulty in Italy, Austria and most other
Catholic countries because of the weak position of the popes.

In France, it was due to Rousseau that the problem assumed the
proportions of a major debate. Advocating an ideal of the state more
totalitarian and exclusive than anything that had been conceived
and propagated before, Rousseau recognised that it was impossible
for Christianity and the Catholic church, because of their inherent
character, to play the role of moral guardians only. Taking the side
of the state, he was concerned with resolving the old clash of interests between it and the church. His ideal state involved the
necessity of wielding the widest possible powers. Religion must
adjust itself to this concept, and the importance that Rousseau
attached to religion was expressed in his *Contrat social* where he
wrote: 'Without religion no people has ever survived or shall survive'. His view that the state could only tolerate the principles of his
own *'religion civile'* and must expel any supra-national, all-embracing
form of Christianity, derives from the state-centred character of
democracy. This idea of the state was opposed in Rousseau's scheme
by an equally strong, uncompromising church. His attitude involved
an ultimate confrontation of the problem of the democratic state and
church. The *religion civile* challenged the state because it had discarded religion and was tolerant only through religious indifference.
His concept of the state was too important to him for religion to be
allowed a free reign, whatever its beliefs. For him – and here
Rousseau went beyond enlightened absolutism and came close to
Jansenism – religion was to such an extent a co-determining element
of the state that both must form a unity. It was evident to Rousseau,
as he described it in the last chapter of the *Contrat social,* that the
religion he envisaged could not be Catholicism, and indeed, this
book, published as early as 1762, was a fierce attack on the Catholic
church. But the attack was directed, as many people realised, against
the church of the Roman pope and not against the episcopal national

IL TRIONFO della SANTA SEDE

E DELLA

CHIESA

contro gli assalti de' Novatori

combattuti e respinti colle stesse loro armi.

OPERA

di

D. MAURO CAPPELLARI

Monaco Camaldolese

ORA

GRECORIO XVI.

Sommo Pontefice

IN VENEZIA

Nella Casa del Tipografo Editore

Giuseppe Battaggia

1832

churches which had entered into close alliance with the state. As the general trend of the times seemed directed towards enhancing the omnipotence of the state, Rousseau's ideas had great explosive force. They were based, however, on two extremes: on an ideal state, the form of which was then hardly recognisable, and on a church with evident Gallican traits. Rousseau regarded the church as an independent and unalterable power in relation to the monarchy and its privileges in ecclesiastical matters, though integrated in and linked with the state. With such premises a compromise was indeed difficult to achieve. The question was only whether these extreme positions bore any relation to reality. This was doubted by many, especially among the French clergy. Significantly many Italian sympathisers with the Jansenists saw Rousseau's system less as a fundamental attack upon the church than as an attempt to integrate a reformed Catholic church into a new pattern of society. They, too, were unable to take the anti-clerical core of Rousseau's doctrine seriously.

Yet the clash between the church and the French Revolution was hardly influenced by Rousseau's theories. Indeed, at the beginning everything was done to avoid and overcome possible opposition and to get on with the experiment of fusing church and state. It was only the later conflict which seemed to confirm Rousseau's theory, and which produced the biased view of 'Rousseau's democracy' as the implacable enemy of the Catholic church. The effects of this prejudice are still felt.

The process of merging Catholic church and state which began when Third Estate and clergy constituted the National Assembly, underwent various stages. At the outset there was the desire to reform, almost to remodel, not only the state but also the church, by abolishing the privileges of the episcopate and thus of the whole Gallican system, and by simultaneously handing over important administrative functions to church and clergy. Catholicism was to become the established religion of France, state and church were to form an inseparable entity. This project had the enthusiastic support of a broad section of the clergy and of some of the bishops; the *Constitution civile* was its ultimate expression. In view of the responsibilities which the clergy assumed in French local government organisation and which were later to be increased, it was a natural development for priests to become civil servants, particularly since after the confiscation of church property the remuneration of the clergy had to be settled anew. As officials, however, they became dependent on the state and on its new rulers. Even this might have been tolerated if the clergy's ecclesiastical functions had remained dominant. The clash became unavoidable when, on 13 April 1790 the National Assembly rejected the proposal to proclaim Catholicism as the national religion. It would have added to the clergy's administrative functions to such an extent that very little of their priestly office would have remained. The clergy therefore no longer felt itself able to support the Civil Constitution by which, for example, bishops and clergy would have been appointed by political bodies. A majority in the French church now refused to take the oath on the Civil Constitution. A deep gulf divided the two camps in the church. Radicalism and attacks on Christianity increased in the general revolutionary atmosphere, driving the priests and bishops who supported the Constitution into a position which seemed to justify Rousseau's claim that democracy and the Catholic church could not be reconciled. At the same time the support which Pius VI gave to those who refused the oath proved a powerful aid for them.

While this conflict was ascribed later to Rousseau's ideas, and Catholics came to accept a basic antagonism between democracy and their church, much of this first important collision was accidental. Both sides were much more concerned with the actual situation than with the theory behind it. After all it was not for the first time that enemies of the church among enlightened thinkers had shown little understanding of the ecclesiastical and religious aspects of the problem. When, several months after the rejection of the Civil Constitution by the French clergy, and following the first persecutions, Pius VI condemned the revolutionary regime, his move was widely regarded as justified since he was condemning men who had also rejected and ridiculed all previous concepts of social order. Considering the structure of the curia and its attitude toward the Enlightenment, it could hardly be expected to adopt a balanced attitude towards the volcanic eruption of the French Revolution. It was only later that the principles behind the conflict as well as Rousseau's theories came to be regarded as the main motives. At the time it certainly did not appear that the democratic republican system must always be equated with the events of 1790 in France and that no other pattern of democracy beside the French one was possible. The question of whether the oppression of conscience as practised by the French Revolution was conditioned by its institutions or by historical circumstances never arose. The fact that the problem of church and state caused further conflicts throughout the nineteenth century merely confirmed the view concerning their incompatibility, and naturally no Catholic made the allowances for revolutionary regimes which he granted to monarchies as a matter of course.

While in France the way was prepared for a fundamental clash between democracy and Catholicism, a new relationship between state and church developed across the Atlantic which disproved the belief that these powers could not be reconciled. The separation of church and state in north America had been effected not because the subjection of the church had proved impossible, as in France, but because no other course was open to those who had left Europe to escape religious intolerance and who wished to defend the Protestant idea of Christian liberty. Church and state were separated, not through religious indifference, but because Christianity was considered to be the natural premise of the American constitution. It could therefore be left to the individual to decide which religion he would adopt. The dissemination of a non-Christian religion in America would have been unthinkable, at least in the early decades. But America was part of the Protestant world and differed too much in all its circumstances to offer Europeans a solution for their more urgent problem of the omnipotent modern state and the Catholic church.

2 The triumph of the papacy

The phoenix papacy

Among the traumatic experiences of eighteenth-century Rome two in particular profoundly affected the following century. There was the fear that national churches might break away from their dependence on Rome, and there was the new antagonism towards the world at large from which the Counter-Reformation had been immune, but which was to become a great danger for the church in the nineteenth century. No one can say what would have happened if the French Revolution had not discredited all the ideas, plans and hopes of the eighteenth century in such a way that the era of Restoration resulted from it. Welcomed with tremendous enthusiasm throughout Europe, the Revolution soon became an object of horror and a justification for all the forces hostile to the times.

This gave the papacy the opportunity for its triumph. It was able to overcome other competing elements within the church, and could do so quite independently of the quality of the theology upheld by the curia. Gradually from the beginning of the nineteenth century the papacy achieved a position that it had never before held in its history, and it did this, not by adapting itself to the spirit of the age, but by skilful manipulation of circumstances. This achievement was a decisive factor for the papacy throughout the nineteenth century. In this the papacy's very hostility towards the age proved one of its strongest weapons. Even before the Revolution the efforts of the Enlightenment to limit the excesses of baroque devotions had been opposed by the popes, and had created unrest and resistance among the lower clergy and the faithful. This harmony of interests between Rome and the Catholic faithful led to an impressive victory for the papacy in the struggle for the Civil Constitution of the clergy. It became clear that when it came to a conflict between papacy and bishops, the latter could count on no support from the faithful.

But this coming triumph seemed remote at the turn of the century and it required Capellari's acute mind to detect any chance at all for future progress in the general confusion.

When, on 29 August 1799, after years of humiliation inflicted upon him by the leaders of the French Revolution, Pius VI died in Valence in the south of France, the end of the papacy seemed to have come. It was impossible to hold a conclave in Rome, which had just been declared a republic. But in accordance with the instructions prudently drawn up by Pius VI one year before his death, a decimated band of 35 cardinals assembled for the conclave at the church of San Giorgio, Venice, from which cardinal Barnabà Luigi Chiaramonti emerged on 14 March 1800 as Pope Pius VII. The new pope was not a strong personality. But in the circumstances of this conclave a strong man could not have become pope without annoying all kinds of governments and thus blocking the chances of the pontificate from the outset. Having been elected under Austrian suzerainty, Pius VII was at once forced to try to obtain the recognition of France, the dominating power, so as not to have to remain confined to the Austrian lands and to court the danger of a schism. Though unassuming in appearance, he had a certain aptitude for his task. In 1797, the French troops had marched on what was then his diocese of Imola, but he had remained at his post and caused a sensation by preaching a sermon in which he declared that the democratic government of the Cisalpine Republic was not contrary to Gospel principles. He told his people to accept the facts of the situation: 'Try to be good Christians and you will become good democrats. Try to imitate the Redeemer's obedience and humility by submitting to the laws and to legal authority.' Although Chiaramonti had thereby incurred the displeasure of the custodian powers, they could not really accuse him of servility towards the new masters. His election as pope thus opened up opportunities for a reconciliation with the ruling powers which he used resolutely and skilfully.

Pius VII was a man of mild disposition and ready to compromise, but he did show admirable firmness in his troubled pontificate. He always endeavoured to protect and defend the rights of the church. In the years of his conflict with Napoleon, however, he was unable to free himself from the influence of the conservative members of the curia and was thus forced to do much that went against his will. He found an ideal secretary of state in cardinal Consalvi, and this team proved as brilliant for church and papacy as that of Leo XIII and Rampolla was to be later in the century. Pius VII's first task was to assert his authority vis à vis Austria and Naples which, after the French defeats in the war of the Second Coalition, had divided the States of the Church among themselves. The pope's return to Rome was made possible only through the French victory at Marengo (14 June 1800), when Napoleon restored to him the area of Rome and the territories up to Fermo. Pius VII had succeeded in obtaining re- cognition from both sides more quickly than expected. The first great event of his pontificate was the concordat of 1801 with France, through which the pope freed himself from the conservatives and made contact with the forces of the future. The significance of this concordat for the papacy can hardly be overestimated.

It was a double triumph. The rulers of France, with Napoleon Bonaparte as their head, acknowledged the failure of their plans to dechristianise France, to found a new secular religion, and to es- tablish a national church independent of Rome by close association of clergy and state. In the concordat, in addition, all the privileges and special feature of Gallicanism were abolished. The conditions for the Catholic church in France were agreed upon between the government and Rome with the episcopate excluded. It was the end of the alliance, so dangerous for Rome, between bishops and government. The curia and not the national episcopate now became the negotiating partner. Even in France, where the curia's influence had hitherto been confined to a minimum, there was henceforth to be no authority in religious questions other than Rome.

Pius VI, exiled by Napoleon from Rome,
is greeted by the populace at Grenoble in 1799.
He died soon afterwards at Valence on 29 August 1799.

The decline of the papacy in France and Germany

The victory of the papacy over the French episcopate was finally
embodied in the agreement that both the government and Rome
would depose both those bishops who had supported, and those who
had refused to support, the Civil Constitution. After some protests
and the refusal to resign by thirty-six of the eighty surviving bishops,
the whole French hierarchy was dissolved on 29 November 1801. The
pope nominated sixty new bishops in consultation with Napoleon.

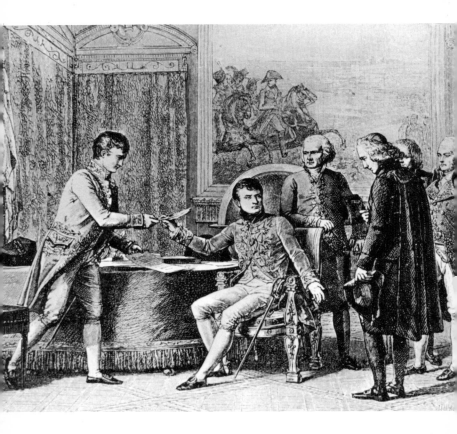

Rome had never before exercised such authority over the French episcopate. Until then bishops were elected, under the king's influence, by cathedral chapters and confirmed by the pope, but the new measure established a relationship between episcopate and papacy that left the former hardly any freedom of movement. Both in France and Germany this caused its importance to become a mere shadow of its former self. Episcopalism, a matter of heated debates in the eighteenth century, had become a dead issue. The pope was no longer *primus inter pares* with special prerogatives, but the bishops' superior who could even deprive them of their office.

It would be wrong to ascribe this settlement to a modern and en-

Napoleon signing the concordat of 1801 in which
he and the pope agreed on a settlement disregarding
the rights of the French bishops. It foreshadowed
the future concordat policy of the Holy See
and the gradual erosion of episcopal rights
in relation to papacy and state.

lightened attitude on the part of the curia, and to maintain that the form it took was what was aimed at. It was the result of lengthy negotiations, frequently at breaking point, in which Consalvi first showed his diplomatic skill. The Paris negotiations of 1801 were decisive for his whole career. In Paris he was faced with problems that seemed to him to open up entirely new possibilities for the papacy. The negotiations for a concordat with Germany, which began some years later, showed that these possibilities were clearly recognised by Consalvi and the curia. Even though the outcome of the French concordat cannot be said to have been planned and foreseen in all details by the church, she quickly realised the advantages offered by the exclusion of the episcopate. This wholly positive result was not diminished by those articles with which Napoleon managed unilaterally to increase the rights of the state.

In Germany a very similar problem had arisen. The process of the secularisation of church property – inevitable after the Congress of Rastatt of 1798 – was bound to revolutionise the structure of the German church. The bishops' loss of temporal power put an end to what they might have hoped for from their own aggrandisement. Rome had no objections to secularisation in Germany where this meant the abolition of the secular territorial powers of the German episcopate.

But secularisation involved more than just the expropriation of spiritual princes. Catholic citizens were transferred to the rule of Protestant princes; the monastries and universities that were dissolved amounted to an unprecedented destruction of Catholic institutions. Until 1803, through its close constitutional links with the spiritual princes, the German Empire had been governed like a Catholic nation; after 1806, and without any changes whatever in the denominational structure, it seemed to be a predominantly Protestant country.

From the Roman point of view the dangerous aspect of seculari-

Pius VII handing the concordat of 1801 to his secretary of state, cardinal Consalvi, who had negotiated it with Napoleon in Paris. Because the cardinal refused to be present at the marriage of Napoleon and Marie-Louise he was banished and dismissed from office. He was reinstated after the fall of Napoleon.

sation in Germany was that the prince primate Karl Theodor von Dalberg, a friend of Napoleon, was the only spiritual prince remaining. In the years after 1805 the curia was worried that Dalberg might become the founder of a German national church largely independent of Rome. Rome therefore spared no efforts to oppose Dalberg's attempts, during Napoleon's coronation in 1804, to obtain papal recognition as primate of Germany. One of Pius' closest counsellors went so far as to tell Dalberg without equivocation that, after the removal of the old, and for Rome dangerous, German and French church organisation, the curia would never again tolerate the establishment of national episcopal structures. Neither in the last years of the Empire nor under the new Rhenish Federation, was Dalberg able to play a role as the last spiritual prince, the organiser of a new Catholic system in Germany or indeed to stop the decline of the church in Germany. After 1803 Rome preferred to leave the German situation obscure for nearly twenty years. No bishops were appointed, no priests were ordained, and in many areas where the incumbent had died, pastoral functions almost ceased. These after-effects of secularisation were particularly unpleasant for Catholics from the formerly Catholic areas who were now expected to submit to Protestant rulers. After the Napoleonic wars, bishop Ignaz Heinrich von Wessenberg, Dalberg's coadjutor at Constance, attempted to save intact some of the church districts of the old Empire, but he too met with Rome's hostility and incurred quite unjustified attacks on his character. The bishoprics with old traditions were quite deliberately eliminated or discriminated against when it came to the reconstruction of the German ecclesiastical organisation, which had of course to follow the pattern of the new political boundaries. Trier and the cathedral city of Mainz, linked for centuries with the history of the empire, were turned into small suffragan-bishoprics; Worms and Constance, the largest diocese in the old Empire, disappeared altogether. As in the

case of France, the changes were carried out in the years 1817 to 1829 by means of concordats and ecclesiastical treaties between Rome and the monarchs concerned. It was not even necessary, as in France, to remove any of the bishops, for they had all died or, like bishop Clemens Wenzeslaus of Trier and Augsburg and the aged bishop Stubenberg of Eichstätt, were easily persuaded to resign. Some, like archbishop Spiegel of Cologne were used to accommodating themselves to demanding governments and submitted

Pius VII looks on helplessly as Napoleon
snatches the Imperial crown and places it on his
own head in Notre Dame, Paris, on 2 December
1804. This gesture, intended to symbolise the
supremacy of the temporal over the spiritual order,
was unprecedented in history.

wholly to the curia. The age of the proud German prelates accustomed to asserting their authority in Rome was past. As in France the bishops had become papal officials.

The conflict with Napoleon

The rise of the papacy after the Napoleonic wars was not, however, due only to the changes in Germany and France by which the middle or 'grey' zone lost its independence. It was also influenced by the treatment which the Pope had suffered under Napoleon. Pius VII, as distinct from his curia, would have been prepared for compromise with Napoleon in the same way that he was ready to compromise in the negotiations with Dalberg. Napoleon well knew why he should keep him away from secretaries of state like Consalvi and, later, Pacca. The concordat signed with Napoleon on 25 January 1813 served to commemorate the wounds which Napoleon had inflicted on Pius VII by arresting him in 1809. For his part, Pius VII by this act of oblivion rendered a service to church and papacy which was of signal importance for the anti-clerical nineteenth century.

Napoleon was compelled to learn the same lesson as his revolutionary predecessors. Thinking that he could reduce the pope's status to that of a court chaplain, he discovered, as did other persecutors of the church before him, that using violence against the pope merely served to add to his triumph. After 1809 Napoleon again resorted to threats and stratagems which he had already employed to get the concordat of 1801. By means of a National Council headed by his uncle, cardinal Fesch, he tried in 1811 to threaten a schism, but this was no longer a serious threat. Governments in modern times could harass the church organisation of their countries to a certain degree, but they could do this only with, and never against, the papacy, which had its firmest allies among their own Catholic citizens.

After the fall of Napoleon, the triumph of the papacy was a

certainty, although it had only indirectly contributed towards his downfall. However, among the forces and powers which had collided with Napoleon, the papacy had emerged as his most consistent opponent. At some time or other all of them, not least the Emperor of Austria, host to the monarchs of Europe at the Peace Congress of Vienna, had compromised with Napoleon and betrayed their principles. It was Pius VII who had opposed the marriage between the Austrian archduchess Marie-Louise and Napoleon and in consequence had suffered arrest and five years' imprisonment in France.

Cardinal Consalvi was the pope's representative at the Congress of Vienna and succeeded in securing the restoration of the Papal States to the Holy See. He governed the Papal States liberally and humanely but gave priests an unprecedented influence in all important offices, thereby causing the incurable antagonism between the clergy and the laity which hastened the end of the papacy's temporal power.

The Papal States restored

Pius VII sent Consalvi, who for several years had also been Napoleon's prisoner, to Vienna. The papacy could have had no better advocate, but it was not an easy task that awaited him. The papacy's increased prestige was offensive to many of the princes and ministers assembled in Vienna, not least to Talleyrand, the representative of France, whom Napoleon had made Prince of Benevento and had given land that was formerly papal territory. Consalvi's mission was made more difficult still because of two measures which the assembled sovereigns and ministers considered an affront. Influenced by Pacca, Pius VII had, on 7 August 1814, decreed the universal restoration of the Society of Jesus, and a few days later he reaffirmed the bull by which Freemasons were excommunicated. Consalvi himself regretted the timing of this as a step likely to jeopardise the position of the pope since many ministers and sovereigns attending the Congress of Vienna were Freemasons. The *ancien régime* and its view of state and church was by no means a dead issue at the Vienna conference table.

At first, therefore, the Congress refused to restore the States of the Church to the pope. It was suggested that certain territories should be made over to him as a gift, but this Consalvi opposed. He would not have the papacy receive the *patrimonium Petri* as a favour from the great powers. He wanted to uphold the ancient papal claim to the States of the Church and demanded their restoration as a matter of right. In long drawn out negotiations Consalvi managed to get this claim accepted. Eventually the larger part of the States of the Church including Benevento was given back to the pope. Some of the northern parts, Comacchio among them, and the area of Avignon and Venaissin in the south of France, were thus lost to Austria.

Thus the Papal States had again risen out of the ashes, but the problematic nature of the papacy's temporal possessions became apparent soon after 1815, and they certainly undermined the pope's prestige. Contrary to the assurances which Consalvi was forced to give in Vienna, the conditions of the *ancien régime* were ruthlessly reimposed. This was carried out by order of the papal protonotary, Rivarola, and cardinal Pacca, the pro-secretary of state. The Papal States had been notoriously badly governed in the eighteenth century; after 1815 they were reputed to be the worst governed country apart from the Ottoman Empire in Europe.

Consalvi was able to establish contacts at the Congress of Vienna which proved most useful in securing the papacy's gains in the eyes of other nations. He stubbornly resisted all attempts by Louis XVIII to renew the Gallican privileges of the French church and to return to the concordat of 1516. This was a decisive achievement. Concordats were concluded with Piedmont (1817) and Naples (1818) in which Consalvi, in contrast to the curia's continued insistence on papal prerogatives, tacitly renounced all papal rights of control in both these kingdoms. Consalvi merely safeguarded the papal right to have a decisive say in episcopal nominations; he did this also in the concordats with Bavaria (1817), Prussia (1821) and in the negotiations successfully concluded in 1829, on the setting up of the church province of the Upper Rhine which was to include Baden, Württemberg, Hessen-Darmstadt, Electoral Hesse and Nassau. There was some trouble in Bavaria when high state officials, and therefore bishops also, were required to swear an oath on the Constitution, as was already customary in France, Württemberg and Baden. But this was a mere formality only remotely comparable to the oath of 1791 in France. Consalvi's diplomacy helped to smooth over all difficulties. These negotiations, however, proved that the popes were no longer dealing with a world favourably disposed towards them. France, Bavaria and Prussia followed the example of Napoleon, who in 1801 had changed the content of the concordat in his favour. All Consalvi's equanimity was needed to prevent the anger which this aroused in the curia from leading to renewed conflicts with the governments concerned. He had to beg Pius VII several times not to give in to the pressure of the conservative cardinals who wanted the negotiations to be broken off.

By means of these treaties, some of which were concluded by his successor, Consalvi laid the basis for a renewed Catholic church with the papacy in dominance as it had never been before. This clearly went against the trend of the times, for the century of nationalism had begun, and such an increase of universal power amidst the growth of national identity was bound to create trouble. Yet the significance of Consalvi's leadership for the church cannot be overestimated, since the continued existence of national church organisations in the age of nationalism might equally have endangered the unity of the Catholic church.

The papacy's declining political influence

The new position of the papacy naturally also entailed new obligations. Its rise was largely due to circumstances beyond its own control. There was no intellectual confrontation with the currents of the times. On the contrary, it was regarded in Rome as a special achievement to have stood out against the age and to have rejected its ideas. Indeed, a confrontation seemed quite superfluous since these ideas had after all proved their terrifying destructive power in the French Revolution. It was firmly believed that a reawakening of currents which, as we have seen, were alive within the Catholic church in the eighteenth century, would merely repudiate and imperil the church.

This development had its repercussions among the European States. Piedmont, Naples, Spain and Portugal, no less than parts of Germany and Austria, thought themselves capable of ignoring the ideals of the French Revolution. But these ideas were so powerful that they imperceptibly transformed these states even where change was resisted. The European age of restoration was at regular intervals both shaken and transformed by revolutionary waves.

In the following chapter I shall deal with the primary outcome of this situation. The position of the church was being undermined, she ceased to be a formative influence of the age, and was forced into the very role envisaged for her by enlightened absolutism, a producer of obedient citizens, holding out the promise of a better future to those who lived under bad governments or in misery. The marxist picture of the Catholic church was essentially determined by this attitude, and it was justified to the extent that the nineteenth-century Catholic church had largely become a government appendage. The pope could not alone make decisions on the Catholic religion in individual countries; he had to co-operate with the state. Governments allowed the church only a narrow field of action confined to fostering among the citizens a spirit amenable to their secular masters. Such was the price which the church had to pay for the rise of the papacy.

The conflict between the church and the age, however, had a further consequence bound up with Consalvi's system of concordats. He was primarily concerned with securing the papal primacy against the claims of national churches and episcopates. Persisting in this aim in spite of many humiliations and stratagems, he sometimes had to accept conditions which met with disapproval in the college of cardinals. Later these treaties took on the significance of a final settlement of church and state relations, though there was less regard for the privileged position which the treaties conceded to the popes – their status came to be accepted as natural; it was rather the content of the treaties that was emphasised in the sense of a legal settlement of the links between the church and individual states. The treaties thus acquired a completely new significance, giving the church some independence from the state, but also legalising situations which could not be considered as the right or the most favourable ones for the church at all times. This approach was in keeping with the old tradition of Roman and curial law, but it prevented the curia from meeting particular situations flexibly and on their merits. Consalvi wanted to secure a position for the popes that he regarded as just and necessary; in fact, as a centralised institution the papacy lost the capacity to adjust itself to the particular situation of individual countries. Consalvi's attitude was conditioned by the eighteenth-century alliance between bishops and absolute rulers which threatened to drive the popes back to a position that would have left them little more than their supremacy in matters of faith. It was only through the unexpected loyalty which the faithful showed the papacy in the French Revolution, in Napoleonic times and throughout the nineteenth century, that the popes were freed from this threat.

This development was accelerated by two further factors on which Consalvi had no influence. One was the backwardness of theological studies in the curia, the other was the repercussions of the restoration of the Papal States.

None of the aims of Reform Catholics had been, as I said, acceptable to the popes. Their newly acquired position, however, needed an intellectual basis. It was understandable enough that, after the fiasco of Reform Catholicism, nobody in Rome had the slightest inclination to resurrect any of its ideas, although they could have been discussed in the post-1815 climate free from pressure and without the danger of either side being forced into an extreme position. But Rome did not even feel the need for such a discussion. The church authorities had become too accustomed to dealing with three clearly defined zones. Although most of the intellectual and political decisions in the nineteenth century occurred in what had been the mixed Catholic-Evangelical middle zone, Rome was not prepared to discuss ideas that came from outsiders. The German church historian Döllinger was justified in remarking that papal supremacy in the early nineteenth century had to rely on the support of the most backward of all theologies, that of Italy. This was the situation which produced the long series of condemnations and excommunications of theological schools of every kind, and it received additional significance from the dominating position of the papacy. It is obviously part of the papal teaching office to decide whether or not a theological school has transgressed the boundaries of the creed. But while in the seventeenth and eighteenth centuries such acts of authority did not preclude the development of new ideas, as we have seen in the case of Jansenism, papal hegemony in the nineteenth century helped to reactivate the medieval practice of uprooting any unfamiliar thinking. In the pontificates of Gregory XVI and Pius IX the intellectual atmosphere of Catholicism became stifling as it had never been in the eighteenth century.

While Consalvi was not himself responsible for these disastrous theological consequences, his great diplomatic achievements cannot be divorced from them. To this day, the existence of a Papal State has been justified by the necessity of investing the pope with greater independence in his dealings with secular governments. This was certainly true while the popes found themselves in competition with more or less autonomous local episcopates. After 1814, however, the Papal States proved a heavy liability that raised the popes to the level of local sovereigns and deprived them of the possibility of intensifying the alliance between papacy and faithful and utilising it for the church. To make matters worse, the church was thereby embroiled in the quarrels of the Italian peninsular, especially in the struggle for Italian national independence.

3 Christian democracy

Two trends: the faithful and the liberals

In the first half of the nineteenth century the papacy's encounter with the idea of Christian democracy was threefold. First, it was implied in the strong support which the popes had found among the Catholic faithful during the French Revolution. This link proved its value repeatedly and became one of the pillars of ultramontanism ('beyond the mountains' i.e. the Alps – the term applied to the defenders of papal supremacy in the Catholic church). In the second place, the ideas of enlightenment, discredited though they had become during the French Revolution, were not without influence, and were taken up by liberal Catholicism. In the third place, we have the joint effect of both these trends on the struggle for independence waged in Catholic countries against their non-Catholic oppressors, as in Ireland, in the Belgian revolution of 1830 and in the Polish rebellions of 1830-1, 1848 and 1863. The nationalist struggles in south America have a similar background.

The two first-mentioned trends were closely linked in some countries, but their relationship with one another and with the world was determined by Rome and by the popes. The papalist loyalty of the Catholic faithful and of liberal Catholicism sprang from very different roots. Both sides were more frequently hostile than friendly to one another. The loyalty of the faithful was the expression of a conservative attitude. For the majority of Catholics the pope was more than merely a spiritual head or the most visible embodiment of the church's unity. They looked to him as the guardian of orthodoxy, and this explains why since the beginning of papal absolutism in the Catholic church no movement condemned by the popes had the slightest chance among the mass of the faithful.

Democratic and liberal ideas in Catholicism have thus always had difficulty in obtaining recognition in Rome. Not infrequently they confronted the popes with criticism. While most of the faithful

allowed themselves to be led without question, liberal Catholics were trouble-makers who wanted to know the why and the wherefore and who were not easily brought to obedience. The conservative majority of the faithful, opposed to any new ideas of the age, was not the one to demand reforms. They had no interest in activating the democratic process which is so characteristic of liberal Catholicism.

The idea of merging church and state in a Christian democratic system had been destroyed by the French Revolution and could not easily be revived. After the reign of terror no one was naïve enough to expect any amelioration from the overthrow of existing conditions. On the other hand, the new position of the popes with regard to awakening nationalism required internal justification. The close alliance between the faithful and the reformed papacy offered itself as a solution.

The new position of the popes was not, however, as we suggested, accompanied by any new act of self-criticism or understanding. The development was accepted in Rome as a matter of course, but

Irish rebels forging pikes during the abortive
rising of 1848 of the so-called 'Young Ireland'
party. This party, chiefly composed of Protestant
journalists and men of letters, had separated
from Daniel O'Connell and became known as the
'Physical Force Party'.

the college of cardinals was divided in its reactions. There were
those who believed that the new church settlement brought about
by Consalvi in France and Germany was paid for by too many concessions to the governments concerned. On the other side were
Consalvi's supporters who considered that the strengthening of the
pope's position justified such concessions. They regarded the concordats as the most important means for the church's development
in a world indifferent to religion, and also as providing guarantees
against the rise of new national churches. Consalvi's opponents,
too, were not interested in securing for the church a position in the
state which would produce new social patterns. They preferred that
the church, with its rights guaranteed, should continue in the same
defensive attitudes towards the state as the curia had adopted in
the eighteenth century. They lacked also any understanding of the
dominant currents of the age, as was shown only too clearly in the
cardinals' reactionary policy of administration in the Papal States.

This attitude made no use of the potential for moral leadership
which Pius VII especially had acquired among Catholics by his stand
against Napoleon. Appeal was made to the traditional authorities
without anyone questioning whether they had been shaken or
whether the church did not owe much less to them than to her loyal
supporters. As seen from Rome, the world had not changed very
much since 1789. It was taken for granted that after the storms
of revolution and after Napoleon, mankind would again accept the
church's values; at the most, it was regretted that this realisation
seemed not to be universal.

The Traditionalists in France

Things were very different in France, where the national catastrophe
favoured a mood of self-examination, the more so since the accepted
institutions of monarchy and state had been radically attacked by

the philosophy of enlightenment. The church was alone in having lost nothing of her magnetism. She had voluntarily surrendered her ties with the ramshackle monarchy, and had courageously resisted the attempts of revolutionaries and of Napoleon to subject her wholly to the state. The end of Gallicanism and the resulting closer links with Rome encouraged the notion of seeing the papacy as the new force of international order. After all, the church had denuded herself of all her riches, and was confronted by a state which, though indifferent to religion, insisted on its sovereign rights over her. Although the French government had no Roman support for the planned re-introduction of the Gallican Articles, it nevertheless again appealed to them.

In this situation a second attempt was made at founding a new social order based on the link between state and Catholic church. The starting point was not very different from that of 1789, even though the ideas developed in violent opposition to the French Revolution. Again it was a matter of equating state and society; the basic question was whether a state inspired wholly by Catholic principles was capable of solving the social problems of the times. But in contrast and in reaction to the rationalism of the French Revolution, the so-called Traditionalists denied the possibility of perceiving truth by reason alone. They assumed an original divine revelation made to mankind which the church preserved as a tradition. Without close links with the church, it was held, state and society could not exist. Based on this premise, the Traditionalists sought to invest the papacy with a dominant role within and above the state. The link with the pope inspired their hope that his authority might restrain the sovereign powers of neo-absolutism. They had no trust in the powers of constitutions to achieve this, and they also opposed man's satanic presumption of acknowledging the guidance of reason alone. The Traditionalists thus became the founders of ultramontanism. The very term signified the changes that had occurred in the former middle zone. The pope was no longer at the centre of world events, but 'beyond the mountains'.

To a certain extent this doctrine reflected the new position of the popes in the church. Traditionalists like De Maistre, Bonald and Lamennais started from a radical negation of the Revolution and the ideological forces behind it. The founder of ultramontanism, Joseph-Marie Comte de Maistre (1754-1821), regarded these forces as works of the devil. He saw in them a punishment which God had inflicted on France, brought about by the victimisation of the Catholic church through Gallicanism, and the moral decline of the *ancien régime* and of its prevailing conditions. It seemed to him that with the Revolution a new age had dawned. The ideas of enlightenment must be rejected outright and the church again be restored to her position at the centre of all intellectual and political decisions – failing that, mankind would go down in further terrible catastrophe. De Maistre was a monarchist. But it was precisely because he saw that the real causes of the catastrophe of the French Revolution lay in absolutism no less than in enlightened deism and its doctrine of man as the measure of all things, that he felt he had to base the renewal of society on two pre-conditions. First, on a structure of the state so firmly anchored in the teaching of the Catholic church that church and state would form an inseparable unity. Secondly, on a limitation of the sovereignty of rulers by the pope. De Maistre developed his doctrine impressively in his great work *Du Pape* (1819), continued under the significant title *De l'Église Gallicane dans son rapport avec le Souverain Pontife* (1821).

The problems he dealt with were very similar to those discussed before the French Revolution towards the end of the eighteenth century which concered the limitation of the power of an absolute monarchy in danger of degeneration. He assumed that man, being evil by nature, cannot arrive at truth by the use of reason by itself. The course of the French Revolution seemed to him to confirm this assumption and he therefore regarded democracy and republicanism as no less diabolical than the Revolution. He thought that his ideal was realised in the restored Bourbon monarchy and its emphatic support for the church, even though he soon found cause to criticise this regime's Gallican tendencies and its indifference towards the Holy See.

Louis Gabriel Ambroise, Vicomte de Bonald (1754-1840), used De Maistre's monarchist ideas to construct a system of more permanent validity, for he started from the premise that state and church were unchangeable entities of which any alteration must necessarily be disastrous. In his view, too, the required unity of powers was to be realised only in a Catholic monarchy. Both De Maistre and Bonald believed in the possibility of a purged *ancien régime* capable of overcoming all its negative features through closer links with the Catholic church. This was also advocated initially by the Breton priest Hughes Félicité Robert de Lamennais (1782-1854), who was perhaps the greatest of these three writers. In his work *Essai sur l'indifférence en matière de religion (1817)*, the first volume of which brought him immediate fame, Lamennais embarked upon a grandiose defence of church and papacy. Like De Maistre, he demanded the recognition of the infallible authority of pope and church. In his second volume (1820), he denied that it was possible to arrive at the true faith by the use of reason alone. According to him, there were two sources, a primal revelation granted by God to the first men, and the *sens commun,* reason and experience in general. These ideas evoked the hostility of the Jesuits. Lamennais, however, was at that time the undisputed leader of French Catholicism. He used his growing influence to support papal centralisation and hailed the pope as the man who had defended the rights of nations against Napoleon's despotism. In his early work there were already traces of the democratic ideas that were soon to be increased.

The doctrines of these Traditionalists met with a mixed reception in Rome. The curia was gratified by their courageous defence of its interests, but at the same time the proposed supremacy over secular rulers which the Traditionalists demanded was felt to be a dangerous exaggeration. Theological objections were soon also raised against the thesis concerning primal revelation and *sens commun*. The Jesuits especially opposed it. Rome procrastinated.

Moreover, to consider and discuss seriously new ideas coming from the alien middle zone was far from being the Roman practice. There was the old suspicion that Protestant thought could thereby be introduced, and in any case the old institution of the curia was not prepared to draw particular conclusions from the closer links with Rome of France, Belgium and Germany and from the ultramontane movement as a whole. Catholic countries like Italy, Spain and Portugal which did not indulge in such extremes were still closer to curial hearts.

Nor, indeed, was Rome in any way prepared for the role which De Maistre assigned to the papacy. Rome clung to the old order of society which was considered to be as secure as many of the results of the Congress of Vienna.

Lamennais: from conservative to liberal

Unlike De Maistre and Bonald, however, Lamennais would not tolerate the resurgence of Gallicanism. The discrepancy between the enlightened indifference of the monarchy and the Gallican claims had not escaped him. He saw that the French monarchy was not Christian in the real sense, but that it regarded the Christian religion only as an administrative instrument and not as the basis of its system. He wrote: 'Being without faith, but convinced of the necessity of some religion to strengthen its authority and procure obedience, the government wants to bring about two things at the same time: a law considered to be divine which binds all subjects,

Félicité Robert de Lamennais, founder of Catholic liberalism and father of Christian Democracy. He was supported initially by Leo XII and Pius VIII, but condemned in 1832 by Gregory XVI. The breach with Rome drove him into the extreme socialist revolutionary camp and he died on 27 February 1854, almost forgotten, in great poverty, and unreconciled with church.

and a church which commands the people but which herself is commanded by the government'. In another even more outspoken passage he described the Bourbon monarchy as having in the same way betrayed church and revolution, for the state-church system was, according to Lamennais, indifferent as regards the nature of the church, and used her only as a means to self-preservation:

> The revolutionaries want freedom without the Church – and they create conditions of anarchy; the restoration regime, still clinging to Gallicanism, aims at a political order as an end in itself, without regard for the general well-being of society, only for the sake of power; it therefore leads to despotism and thus to anarchy.

Lamennais became increasingly hostile to Gallicanism. In 1826 he was fined because of his failure to acknowledge the Gallican Articles of 1682. His trial showed how much the Catholic church in France was again adopting Gallican attitudes. But the new notion of a national church was incomparably more primitive than the one put forward before 1789. While the king was again invested with all the Gallican privileges and the old suspicion of Rome revived, the church had surrendered her former independence vis à vis the state. This was precisely what Lamennais opposed. He accepted the fall of the Bourbon monarchy as inevitable, and concluded that unless the church would sever her links with the monarchy she would go down with it.

In Rome, too, there was concern over the revival of Gallicanism which was rightly regarded as a threat to the papacy. It was for this reason that Leo XII, who had succeeded Pius VII, was much impressed by the ideas which Lamennais had personally explained to him during a visit to Rome in 1824. The pope was known to admire the brilliant French priest and kept his portrait in his study. As an opponent of Consalvi, the pope, like Lamennais, had recognised the ambiguous nature of the church's alliance with the monarchies.

The concordats served their purpose in guaranteeing the freedom of the church and her pastoral function, but in actual fact the church was restricted to the role of moral guardian, which unfortunately seemed to suite the hierarchy. Theology and philosophy had reached the ultimate depths. The advantages that flowed from the alliance between throne and altar were accepted thankfully; the bishops saw themselves as loyal supporters of the monarchy and had no regard for the real nature of the church. Consalvi's settlement of the church-state relationship was achieved at the price of intellectual sterility. The Enlightenment was to blame for everything – that was the simple explanation given by many among the restoration clergy if they thought at all about these matters. And it was believed that only the hard hand of authority could liberate the nation from such evil. In this the clergy relied on the support of a government no less counter-revolutionary in outlook than they were themselves. Social problems were relegated to the field of Christian charity and alms-giving. The belief that man was incapable of reaching perfection was thought a sufficient answer to the imperfections of society.

Against this background Lamennais' vision seemed all the more compelling. There was hardly any theologian of merit in the middle of the nineteenth century who was not influenced by him and his impact when he finally and fully accepted liberalism and democratic republicanism could not have been more sensational.

Like De Maistre and Bonald, Lamennais had started as a fervent royalist but he soon learned that the ideas of the French Revolution were far from vanishing and indeed were finding increasing support, while the monarchy became alienated from its own ideals. He soon came to consider monarchy and revolution merely as different forms of despotism, distinct only in the varying interest of social classes.

With the irrevocable destruction of all privileged and corporate institutions, France, it seemed to Lamennais, had virtually turned republican, even though a king was at its head. In his eyes tyrannical government was the enemy, whether imperial, royal or liberal.

Lamennais' conversion to democracy was also influenced by the struggle of the Irish, Belgians and Poles for independence against their non-Catholic governments. If the close alliance of throne and altar became troublesome in France, the situation was still worse in the case of monarchies which dealt with the Catholic church according to the Protestant model, with open hostility rather than with token respect. In upholding the cause of these nations Lamennais made a special plea for the personal liberty that had always had an important part in his writings. In 1829 he published *Des progrès de la revolution et de la guerre contre l'Église* in which he condemned Gallicanism and, for the first time, called upon the church to form an alliance with the peoples striving for independence.

Lamennais adopted democracy and liberalism in a way wholly typical of him. He was convinced that the truth of Catholicism would finally prevail within a liberal social order and could help towards the interior conversion of the state. The concept of the liberal society became increasingly attractive to him in view of the enslavement of the church by the Bourbon regime.

His reputation was enhanced when, as he had predicted in his book, the Bourbon monarchy fell in 1830. In October 1830 he published the first issue of *L'Avenir*. In this review, soon to become famous, he propagated his ideas on Catholic liberalism and Catholic-liberal co-operation. He chose the motto *Dieu et la liberté,* thus proclaiming his intention of reconciling the Catholic church with the idea of freedom. *L'Avenir* lasted little more than a year, from 16 October 1830 until 15 November 1831, but it was undoubtedly the most important Catholic journal of the nineteenth century. It was less influential in France, where both the anti-clerical monarchy and the Gallican episcopate were against Lamennais, than in Belgium, where Catholic-liberal co-operation as advocated by Lamennais found positive expression in the revolution. There were also enthusiastic supporters in Germany, Ireland and Poland as well as in Italy.

Lamennais' liberalism was a special brand; he believed that because Catholicism reflects God's original revelation, it must necessarily become the decisive spiritual force in a free world. His Catholic liberalism was a transitional phase on the road that led from a society no longer Christian towards one not as yet re-christianised. It was not an end in itself. The church's acceptance of freedom was needed, he felt, if the society of the future was to be shaped by the church. In his view providence had brought about the unconditional alliance between people and church through the collapse of the Gallican church and the rise of the papacy. Lamennais drew up a list of freedoms which seemed to him basic for the new Catholic social order, on which all his hopes were founded. He claimed freedom of conscience and religious worship, freedom of instruction, opinion and assembly. He was no less radical in his political demands: abolition of suffrage based on property qualifications, universal extension of the electoral principle and abolition of the centralisation which was all that remained of Napoleon's despotism. He was also a convinced advocate of self-government. His liberalism, therefore, was not confined to the realm of the church-state relationship. He aimed at a society purged of the political element through a democratic theocracy in which papal supremacy as the guardian of freedom was largely freed from the interference of the state. Awaiting the attainment of this ideal, he demanded the widest possible amount of freedom for the church in society. He wanted to make Catholicism secure through freedom rather than through government support which, he was convinced, could but discredit the church. It followed logically from all this that he should want to separate state and church and terminate the Napoleonic concordats and the remuneration of the clergy by the state. He felt sure that a church completely independent of the state must win back the souls lost to her. He was equally convinced that the liberals of old, the advocates of the revolutionary ideas of 1789 and of religious intolerance would support the Catholic cause, since the freedom which they wanted could not survive without the kind of order represented by the church. His language at that time acquired a passionate intensity. He appealed to Catholics:

Servants of Him who was born in a stable and died on the cross, return to your origins, strengthened again through poverty and suffering! Then the word of Christ will regain its primary effectiveness upon your lips. Descend among the nations without any other support than that of the word of God, like the twelve apostles, and begin again to conquer the world! Christendom is on the threshold of a new era of triumph and glory. See the signs of the new dawn on the horizon. Standing on the ruins of empires and the debris of all transitory things, come and join in the hymn to life!

Lamennais finally shocked Europe by even justifying revolution, and calling to his supporters: 'Freedom must be fought for, it is never surrendered voluntarily'.

It was gratifying for him that this appeal found an enthusiastic echo in Belgium. Catholics and liberals, victims alike of persecution, rose against the regime of king William. Lacordaire, who supported Lamennais and later played a leading part in reforming the French Dominican Order, advocated the complete separation of church and state by pointing to the example of north America. In Belgium, these ideas fell on fertile soil and they found concrete expression in Catholic-liberal co-operation as envisaged by the Belgian constitution. The Belgian clergy and bishops entered the National Assembly as deputies. The liberal constitution was to prove successful. Joyfully Lamennais wrote on 28 June 1821:

It is not that everywhere the Catholic peoples are on the march as though they were the first to have a vision of the future destiny of mankind? The more fervently they believe, the more forcefully they will be able to go forward with raised head, trembling with excitement, on the quest for the great future. Just look to Belgium, Ireland, holy and heroic Poland. I tell you, Christ is there!

In the apathetic atmosphere of Catholicism at the time of the restoration Lamennais evoked tremendous enthusiasm. His reference to the struggle for political independence attained in the name of the church in Belgium, Ireland and Poland might have been completed by the example of the struggle for independence in south America. But unfortunately Leo XII, anticipating the reactionary attitude of Gregory XVI, opted for the old order and managed to turn the initial fervour for Catholicism into that open hostility towards the church which has characterised the south American situation to this day.

Rome's condemnation of Lamennais

Lamennais had evidently not grasped this warning example, for he not only felt that he was at one with the trends of the times, but thought also that he was upholding the ideas and interests of the pope. For a short time he gave to Catholicism an unprecedented revolutionary impetus which in many countries such as Germany was essential to the Catholic renewal. In France Lamennais encountered violent opposition from his wholly Gallican-minded fellow Catholics. Clinging to the old alliance of throne and altar, the French bishops regarded Lamennais as a dangerous revolutionary using his fame to stir up rebellion amongst the faithful. For a long time the bishops failed to realise that he was highly thought of in Rome and he may have to some extent confirmed them in their Gallican anti-Roman attitude. They suspected that by inciting Catholics to rebellion the pope wanted to achieve supremacy over their government. Gallicans and royalists joined forces against the ultramontanism of Lamennais. *L'Avenir* was accused of revolutionary intrigues against the monarchy and many bishops forbade their clergy to read it, as its views, it was alleged, were rejected by Rome. Circulation figures dropped and on 15 November 1831 Lamennais took leave of his readers, saying that it was now for the pope to decide upon his teaching. He wrote:

Our faith has been questioned, and even our views. We are leaving the battlefield for a time in order to fulfil an equally urgent duty. Taking up the pilgrim's staff, we shall be making our way to the eternal pulpit and, cast down at the feet of the High Priest whom Jesus Christ has placed over his apostles as head and master, we shall say to him 'Father, read into our souls, nothing in them shall be hidden from you. If any one of our thoughts, only a single one should go against your own, reject it and we shall abjure it. Father, speak to us the word that gives life because it gives light. May your hand be stretched out towards us blessing our obedience and love'.

At the end of the year, together with his friends Lacordaire and the young Montalembert, who had suggested the fateful journey, Lamennais arrived in Rome. But Leo XII, his benefactor, had been dead for nearly two years, and the short pontificate of Pius VIII, who was probably not unfavourably disposed towards Lamennais, was ending. Fra Mauro of Camaldoli, author of *Il Trionfo della Santa Sede* was elected pope on 2 February 1831 and took the name of Gregory XVI.

Lamennais succeeded in finding support among the young priests in Rome, but in the curia he met with resistance, and in an audience with Gregory XVI the pope gave him no chance to explain his ideas. Apparently unknown to Lamennais, a violent struggle was going on behind the scenes. Many governments, especially that of Metternich, had already exerted pressure on the Holy See to silence the turbulent French priest. When Lamennais left Rome in July 1832, he did not expect an explicit approval of his doctrines, but certainly not their condemnation. He was with friends in Munich,

Gregory XVI giving the blessing 'urbi et orbi'
in St Peter's Square. This traditional blessing
was withheld from 1870 to 1922 to emphasise
the pope's status as 'prisoner in the Vatican'
in the quarrel with the new united Italy
over the Papal States.

among them Görres, Döllinger and Schelling, when the news
was brought to him on 30 August that Gregory XVI, though without mentioning his name, had condemned his theses in the encyclical
Mirari vos of 15 August 1832. They were all dumbfounded.
Lamennais and his friends immediately submitted to the pope's
judgment, but in the long run a breach was unavoidable. In a letter
from Cardinal Pacca, Lamennais was told of the reasons for the
pope's decision. Then in 1834 he raised his voice again, summaris-
ing his ideas about the future liberation of the suffering masses in
his *Paroles d'un croyant*. Some passages in this book were taken to
be a criticism of the Holy See. Gregory's unusually massive counter-
attack came in the encyclical *Singulari nos* of 7 July 1834. In 1836
Lamennais published his passionately bitter onslaught *Affaires de
Rome*, which completed the breach. He left the church. Later he
came out with some pungent socialist revolutionary ideas, but being
outside the church, it no longer mattered what he said. Having rejected his ideas, Rome condemned him to impotence, a fate shared
in the years to come by many other eminent Catholics, Döllinger
among them. Broken in spirit and forgotten by all, Lamennais
died on 27 February 1854. He was buried in a mass grave; his last
resting place is unknown.

From the Roman point of view, there were certainly grounds for
not accepting Lamennais' theses. The whole basis of his traditionalistic approach and its opposition to the possibility of knowing God
was irreconcilable with the teaching of the church: it was in fact
condemned by the First Vatican Council in 1870. But this was not the
true reason for *Mirari vos*. As Gregory told the Austrian ambassador
Count Lützow, he was less concerned with Lamennais, whom he
would gladly have spared on account of his services to the papacy,
than with upholding 'the true principles' of religion which alone
could guarantee the order and stability of society. *Mirari vos*,
Singulari nos and other encyclicals of Gregory XVI and Pius IX up

to the notorious *Syllabus,* are documents expressing the church's rejection of contemporary ideas. These are stages on the road leading into the Catholic ghetto.

Lamennais, for his part, had no doubt whatsoever that the papacy could only have gained by adopting his teaching. But this view was based on a complete misreading of the Roman conditions. Nothing could have been further apart than Rome's ultra-conservatism and Lamennais' aims.

Oddly enough, by 1831 Lamennais had reached the very position held by the Jansenists at the beginning of the French Revolution. They looked to democracy, knowing well that the modern state would merely misuse an absolute power like the church as the guardian of public morality. The Jansenists, like the clerical supporters of the Revolution in 1789, believed in a Catholic state in which society and church formed a unity. But this was the view which Gregory, as Cappellari, had already castigated in 1799 in *Il Trionfo della Santa Sede.* In 1831 the pope was quite unable to understand Lamennais' intellectual background, but he did recognise the results and in them he saw Lamennais aligned with his old opponents, the Jansenists and their allies and the revolutionaries of 1789. The only difference as far as he was concerned was that Lamennais wanted to achieve his aims not against but with the help of the Holy See; in Gregory's eyes this idea was tantamount to sacrilege.

Part 2

The years of
restoration 1831 - 78

The encyclical *Mirari vos* (15 August 1832)
in which Gregory XVI declared his opposition
to the liberal tendencies of his time
(freedom of conscience, freedom of the press,
separation of church and state) and to the
political theories of Lamennais.

In the bull *Mirari vos* Gregory XVI spoke out with all the authority
at his command for the close and insoluble alliance of throne and
altar. It was primarily a political decision, although motivated by
religion. Nations were urged to stand by their monarchs in loyalty.
There is a reference to the early Christians' submission to the pagan
Roman emperors, and the Bull continues:

These fine examples of loyal submission to princes, which necessarily derives
from the sacred precepts of the Christian religion, condemn the detestable
insolence and malice of those who, incited by their vaunting and unbounded
ambition for licentious freedom, use all their power to agitate against and
upset the rights of rulers, whereas they really enslave the nations under the
mask of liberty.

The 'errors of the times', especially indifferentism and the various
freedoms, are condemned in the most violent terms:

From this poisonous spring of indifferentism has also flowed that absurd and
erroneous doctrine or rather, the delirium, that freedom of conscience is to
be claimed and defended for all men. Entrance for this pernicious error is
paved by the complete and unrestrained freedom of opinion which is spreading
everywhere to the ruin of both the church and the state and which many
maintain with supreme insolence is advantageous to religion. But in the words
of St Augustine, 'What is a worse death for the soul than the freedom of
error?' Assuredly, when every restraint which holds men in the pathway of
truth has been removed, our already disordered nature plunges headlong to
disaster and we can truly say that the pit of the abyss has been opened from
which John (Apoc. 9.3) saw smoke rising and obscuring the sun, and locusts
swarming forth and laying waste the earth. Hence the deflection of minds, a
yet deeper corruption of youth, contempt for sacred matters and laws spread
among the nations. Prosperous states have perished through this one evil, the
immoderate freedom of opinions, licence of speech and love of novelties.
Linked with this is that abominable and detestable freedom of publication
which some dare demand with much noise and zeal.

GREGORIUS PAPA XVI

VENERABILES FRATRES

Salutem, et Apostolicam Benedictionem.

Mirari vos arbitramur, quod ab imposita Nostrae humilitati Ecclesiae universae procuratione nondum Litteras ad vos dederimus, prout et consuetudo vel a primis temporibus invecta, et benevolentia in vos Nostra postulasset. Erat id quidem Nobis maxime in votis, ut dilataremus illico super vos cor Nostrum, atque in communicatione spiritus ea vos adloqueremur voce, qua confirmare Fratres in persona Beati Petri jussi fuimus (1). Verum probe nostis, quanam malorum aerumnarumque procella primis Pontificatus Nostri momentis in eam subito altitudinem maris acti fuerimus, in qua, nisi dextera Dei fecisset virtutem, ex teterrima impiorum conspiratione Nos congemuissetis demersos. Refugit animus tristissima tot discriminum recensione susceptum inde moerorem refricare; Patrique potius omnis consolationis benedicimus, qui, disjectis perduellibus, praesenti Nos eripuit periculo, atque, turbulentissima sedata tempestate, dedit a metu respirare. Proposuimus illico vobiscum communicare consilia ad sanandas contritiones Israel; sed ingens curarum moles, quibus in concilianda publici ordinis restitutione obruti fuimus, moram tunc Nostrae huic objecit voluntati.

Noi c'immaginiamo, che Voi vi meravigliate, perchè dopo essersi imposto alla Nostra tenuità l'incarico del governo di tutta la Chiesa, non vi abbiamo per anche indirizzate Nostre lettere, secondo che e la consuetudine fin dai primi tempi introdotta, e la benevolenza Nostra verso di Voi avrebbe richiesto. Era questa per vero dire una delle Nostre più vive brame di dilatare senza indugio sopra di voi il Nostro cuore, e di favellarvi nella comunicazione dello spirito con quella voce, con cui nella persona di Pietro a Noi divinamente fu ingiunto di confermare i Fratelli (1). Ma Voi ben sapete, per qual procella di mali e di calamità fin dai primi momenti del Nostro Pontificato fummo tosto balzati in un mare sì tempestoso, che se la destra del Signore non avesse fatta palese la virtù sua, avreste dovuto per la più perversa cospirazione degli empj compiangere il Nostro fatale sommergimento. Rifugge l'animo dal rinnovare coll'amara esposizione di tanti infortunj il dolore vivissimo, che ne provammo; e più Ci piace di sollevare riconoscenti benedizioni al Padre di ogni consolazione, il quale colla dispersione de' ribelli dall'imminente pericolo ci trasse, e sedata la furiosa tempesta ci fè respirare. Noi ci proponemmo incontanente di comunicare s co voi i Nostri divisamenti alla sanazione intesi delle piaghe di Israele: ma la grave mole di cure, che ne sopraggiunsero per conciliare il ristabilimento dell'ordine pubblico, pose allora un ostacolo a tal Nostro pensiero.

The whole tenor suggests that Gregory had not even understood the ideas of Lamennais. Even cardinal Pacca, certainly no progressive, had his doubts about a statement so strongly in favour of the restoration. But Gregory was not a free man. He felt obliged to speak out because the Revolution was creating so much trouble for him in his own country that on 19 February 1831 he had to appeal for help to the Austrians who, together with the French, moved in to occupy the States of the Church until 1838. Only the protection of foreign bayonets could maintain the clerical regime. The prevailing conditions were not of Gregory's but of Leo XII's making. 'Other popes too incurred hatred, but at least they had some supporters,' wrote Leopold von Ranke, the historian of the papacy. 'But Leo XII was hated by everybody from princes to beggars; nobody was his friend.' The pope on whom Lamennais had based his hopes – it was said that he was about to make Lamennais a cardinal – is revealed on closer inspection to be the worst of Roman reactionaries. What had attracted Lamennais to him was only marginally connected with the Frenchman's ideas. In Leo's perspective the Breton priest was a pawn in his struggle against the Gallican attempts to wrest independence from Rome. Lamennais' enthusiasm, however, was directed towards the institution of the papacy, not towards the man who had assumed office in 1830 and whom he evidently did not know at all. Lamennais felt sure that the papacy, having risen to such heights of prestige, would open up towards the world and its problems and would thus be changed. But it was this precisely which Gregory XVI and the curia contested. In *Mirari vos* it is stated:

For, to use the words of the Fathers of Trent, the church has been instructed by Jesus Christ and his apostles and taught by the Holy Spirit who imparts to her all truths at all times. It would therefore be completely absurd and supremely insulting to suggest that the church stands in need of restoration and regeneration, as though these were needed for her preservation and increased growth, as though she could be exposed to exhaustion, degradation or other defects of this kind.

Lamennais' and Gregory's views on the nature of the church and the papacy were thus utterly irreconcilable. Gregory saw the papacy as an inflexible institution: it was the world that was to blame for its own unbelief and that had to adjust itself accordingly. But popes and priests had only the means of external pressure: admonitions, concordats, treaties, condemnations, bans. As an inflexible institution of this sort the papacy necessarily became the absolute antithesis of the changing society of the nineteenth century.

The conflict with modern society

The clash between the papacy and society occurred for three different reasons, all dependent on one another and interacting. First of all, a basic principle was involved and this tended to increase suspicion of the former 'grey' middle zone. Contrary to the attitude in former centuries, however, and despite many misunderstandings, this area was now emphatically pro-Roman and the continuing Roman suspicion of the bogey of independent national hierarchies was soon to be dispelled. The conflict therefore shifted to those countries where, under the impact of nationalist chauvinism, Roman Catholics became suspected of being unreliable citizens. Rome herself was only involved in so far as she was a retarding factor in the general Catholic quarrel with modern ideas.

Secondly, the Roman reactionary attitude, largely conditioned as it was by the Italian situation, was aggravated by the antagonism between the papacy and the Italian national movement and, later, the unified Italian state. Events in Italy were disastrous in their effects on the policy of the papacy and its attitude towards the modern world. A major factor naturally was the reaction in other

countries to the deplorable regime in the Papal States. The Revolution of 1831 had been largely caused by maladministration. The subsequent Franco-Austrian occupation, which had Gregory's blessing, fanned the hatred of Italian nationalism. 'In court cases liberals were particularly penalised by command of the secretary of state, Bernetti,' writes Schwaiger. 'Discontent was rife among the educated classes, especially since according to the medieval precedent, the rule of canon law was applied also in civil matters. Magistrates' courts imposed fines, even prison sentences, on those found to have eaten meat on Fridays; to inform the authorities of such transgressions was made an obligation under threat of ecclesiastical penalties.'

Gregory XVI had great difficulty in resisting continual outbreaks of revolt in his own territories, even after the foreign troops had left, and this confirmed him in his anti-liberal views and in his opposition to the age. The States of the Church were a heavy liability in the papacy's relations with the modern world.

In May 1835, Gregory XVI travelled for the first time
on a French steamboat from Civitavecchia to Corneto
(now Tarquinia). This was an important occasion for
the unworldly former Fra Mauro who used to say that
railways and steam-traction were the works of Satan:
'chemin de fer, chemin d'enfer' is a remark attributed to him.

Thirdly, there were the internal conflicts in the church, which had
their origin in the revival of theological studies in Gregory's reign.
These were mainly concerned with two issues. There was the attempt
to develop, by way of continuing the baroque theology, a Catholic
philosophy equipped to fight the rationalism of the Enlightenment.
The Jesuits were the main supporters of this neo-scholastic school
which was mainly inspired by Aquinas. It was opposed by another
school with chiefly German support, which sought to reconcile
Catholicism with contemporary trends in philosophy, that is, with
Kant, Hegel, Fichte and Schelling. For a long time both schools had
existed side by side. But the more up-to-date romantic-idealist
theology was from the beginning regarded as suspect in Rome.
Three of its most important philosophical systems were condemned
between 1835 and 1861: Hermesianism, based on the teaching of
Georg Hermes; Güntherianism, based on the philosophy of Anton
Günther; and ontologism, which found support in Belgium, France
and northern Italy. The victory of neo-scholasticism, which was
found attractive in Rome not only because of its conservative and
traditional character, was assured by these condemnations. The
mere fact that the other schools had no Vatican representatives
sufficed to make them suspect at the increasingly centralised head-
quarters of the church. In addition, nationalist accents could be
detected among the theological opponents of scholasticism.
Döllinger, for instance, referred to the superiority of 'German'
theology over other schools owing to the achievements of German
scholarship. Ontologism was turned by its French supporters into
a kind of French national theology. The same thing happened in
Italy where Gioberti, the leader of the ontologists, played a leading
part in the ideological discussions of the *risorgimento*. As against
these schools, neo-scholasticism was the only theological system
common to all countries. Increasing centralisation within the curia
contributed to the strengthening of neo-scholasticism; it was a

pedestrian type of theology, utterly remote from the scientific interests of the time. The proclamation of the dogma of papal infallibility, which was advocated mainly by the neo-scholastics, finally decided the issue.

Although it is certainly true that the Roman curia was at no time in its long history a progressive body, its traditionalist and conservative outlook reached its most extreme in the nineteenth century under the impact of the French Revolution. Conflicts with the age would certainly also have occurred in any similar traditional body. But in the eighteenth century at least there were cardinals with Jansenist leanings and new ideas could still be discussed, whereas nineteenth-century Rome was so violently intolerant that at the very moment when the papacy's newly acquired and unprecedented world position required it to understand the world, it became unfit to do so.

The final tragedy was that, through *Mirari vos* and the institutionalisation of the alliance between throne and altar, Gregory XVI, quite unaware of what his action entailed, committed the Catholic church to remaining tied to the old social structure. Lamennais wanted the Catholic church to welcome a new social order, and to discard the monarchies of the past, but Rome was intellectually quite incapable of seeing in this wish more than a senseless and dangerous revolt against the existing order, of which the church was a part. The sympathies which Leo XII and Pius VIII expressed towards Lamennais were intended neither for the man who had rebelled against an outdated social order, nor for the visionary of a renewed church, but exclusively for one who had supported the new position of the popes and had forcefully written against the Gallican trend in French Catholicism, which in Roman eyes was still the real danger. The church's stubborn commitment to the age of restoration proved a heavy burden, and even Leo XIII could not wholly rid himself of it.

The papacy's rejection of leadership

If the papacy had accepted what Lamennais stood for and rejected the ancient order, it could have become the leader of a revolutionary movement. But where was this movement leading? No one knew the answer. Beyond his own conviction that Catholic truth must ultimately triumph in a liberal world, Lamennais himself was unable to predict the shape of things to come. The Belgian revolution seemed to justify his views. But in order to predict what would happen to countries of a wholly different social structure if they accepted the liberal-bourgeois order, Rome would have needed a capacity for assessing social criteria which no one in the world, least of all the Holy See, possessed at that time. There were no intellectual links between the papacy and the liberal middle classes.

The Christian churches generally had the chance, around the year 1800, of joining in the intellectual, social and political transformation of the age and of exerting a formative and beneficial influence. The Catholic church was in a particularly favourable position because her links with the monarchy and the old social order were not as close as those of Protestantism. Nevertheless, as the example of England shows, the social changes which were linked with industrialisation occurred with fewer upheavals in the Protestant than in the Catholic world, the latter proving less amenable to the rise of modern capitalist society. The Catholic church had the opportunity of exerting an influence beyond national boundaries, a process which necessarily would have made her the saviour of the oppressed everywhere and a force on which the hopes of mankind might have concentrated. Having failed to use this chance, the papacy soon found itself prevented by the fatal alliance of throne and altar from actively intervening in the course of events. It became the great retarding force, yet at the same time powerless to back the monarchies and the old order in the way they wanted. Amidst the great social tensions of the nineteenth century the Catholic church, like the other churches, was bound to fail in the task imposed upon her of merely producing obedient citizens. What Eduard von Hartmann said about the relationship in the nineteenth century of the German Evangelical church to the state also applied to the Catholic church: 'The church wants to reduce the role of the state to that of a police force, the state wants to reduce the role of the church to a wholly dependent association'. The conflict might have been solved by the kind of inter-relationship of church and state such as was frequently attempted after 1789 without finding acceptance, much less understanding, in Rome. The link with the old order was no real alternative to the *aggiornamento*. For, in fact, neither was the old society really prepared to accept the church, nor was the church prepared to accept the role bestowed upon her by that society. Lamennais was right in emphasising the degradation to which the monarchies had subjected the church. They looked upon her merely as a protective shield against revolution, a shield, however, of decreasing value, since the church, by virtue of the link between altar and throne, was progressively losing her influence over the broad masses and it was to this influence that the monarchies wanted to limit her.

The trend of the papal elections in the nineteenth century shows that the equivocal nature of this development was recognised in Rome. The course and outcome of any conclave invariably produced a strong reaction to the preceding reign. Opposition to Consalvi resulted, after the death of Pius VII, in the election of the ultra-conservative Leo XII in 1823. His death in 1829 was followed by the election of the progressive-minded Pius VIII, but he reigned only for eighteen months. Under the impact of the July Revolution and under strong pressure from Metternich, the ultra-conservative Gregory XVI was elected and reigned for fifteen years. After his death a young, open-minded man capable of tackling the difficult tasks of reform was favoured by most of the cardinals. Pius IX,

Cardinal Giacomo Antonelli (1806–76), secretary of state from 1850, exercised an overwhelming influence on Pius IX and was largely responsible for the extreme conservative and intransigent policies of the Papal States and for the pope's obstinate rejection ('Non possumus') of all compromise between the church and the government of united Italy.

thirty-four years old at the time of his election, remained a liberal, however, for only two years. The revolution of 1848 had the effect of turning him into a man whose views strongly resembled those of Gregory XVI whom he had originally criticised. Pius IX governed for thirty-two years. It was only after his death with the election of Leo XIII that a pope was found who set himself earnestly to the task of reconciling the church with the world. With him, it may be said, the papacy began to be a formative factor of the times. The majority in the college of cardinals had expressed their wish at least twice (in 1829 and in 1846) for a change of course, yet in the half century between 1823 and 1878, there were only five years (1829-30 and 1846-8) of papal government by men with positive attitudes towards the world and its problems. Some ultra-conservative cardinal-secretaries of state, among whom Tommaso Bernetti (1828-36), Luigi Lambruschini (1836-46) and Giacomo Antonelli (1850-76) who were notorious for their intransigent reactionary attitudes, added to the general trend. Lambruschini and Antonelli exerted a fatal influence in compelling their sometimes wavering masters to adopt extreme positions. They were primarily responsible for the oppressive regime of the Papal States.

4 The fall of the Papal States

The restoration of clerical rule and absolutism in the Papal States after 1816 was, as I said, one of the worst liabilities which the papacy incurred in the nineteenth century. The Napoleonic administration which, though by no means ideal, was progressive and fair, had sufficed, in less than ten years, to spread deep hatred among the people of the previous order, which was now shown to have had all the worst faults imaginable in any government. The arbitrary and catastrophic regime after Napoleon was not so much caused by Gregory XVI and Pius IX as allowed to grow through ignorance and helplessness, and the new ideas which were soon added to the general discontent made it seem quite intolerable. The Italian movement for unity was based on liberal ideas which made it one of the most exciting sources for intellectual and moral renewal of the nineteenth century. The Italians found for it the appropriate name: the *risorgimento*. The insoluble conflict which soon arose between the Risorgimento and the Papal States, and thus the papacy, was not however inevitable. There had been no lack of attempts to find an honourable place in an Italian confederation for the papacy, which the Italians after three centuries of foreign domination had come to regard as the guardian of their civilisation. The situation became impossible only when Lambruschini and Antonelli blocked every attempt to reform or improve the economic and social conditions in the Papal States, and rejected the incorporation of the *Patrimonium Petri* into the Italian confederation. Both these cardinals considered the Italians a rebellious and atheistic people who must again be taught obedience by discipline, force and punishment. The outcome was that between 1831 and 1870 the popes were only able to survive in their own lands for a few years without the protection of foreign soldiers and indeed their rule came to an end as soon as these troops had left.

The rise of Italian nationalism

Two very characteristic expressions of the movement for Italian unity faced Gregory XVI and Pius IX, and they had a lasting effect on the papal relationships with liberalism and other ideological currents. One was the fervent and zealous nationalism of Giuseppe Mazzini, the other the more detached and realistic approach of Vincenzo Gioberti known as *neo-guelfismo*. Both movements tried to find a philosophical and theological basis for their political ambitions for Italian independence. They were opposed by the popes who, with the scepticism dictated by centuries of experience, were accustomed to look upon Italy as a geographical entity only and refused to the very end to believe in the possibility of an Italian national state. This inflexible opposition, maintained until 1929, to any reconciliation with Italy was for a long time inspired by expectations that the Italian kingdom would disintegrate and the States of the Church rise again. To papal Rome it seemed that a united Italy was a structure too artificial to survive.

Mazzini became increasingly confident that it was his generation's task to undertake the liberation of Italy as a service pleasing to God, a kind of substitute religion, in which nationalism, republicanism and belief in progress formed a strange alliance. Because of this he condemned his own movement to remain within the limits of sectarianism. Not many Italians were prepared to sacrifice the tenets of Catholicism, to which they were especially attached, for this kind of ecstatic vision. Small in numbers, his followers exhausted themselves in countless ill-prepared and suicidal enterprises. On the other hand, Mazzini's movement was distinguished by its lofty moral purpose. The freedom and unity of Italy were not to be attained by compromises but by a renewal affecting all the people. To create one nation, free and able to decide its own destiny, was Mazzini's aim. His democratic republic thus differed essentially from the ideals of the French Revolution in that it primarily looked to the people's moral elevation, with emphasis on fraternal rather than sovereign rule. This approach was conditioned by the Italian situation. He was resolutely against class hatred and social revolution and believed in the possibility of social progress through moral endeavour as an answer to the current socialist ideas which he encountered in their Saint-Simonian form. Mazzini played a special role in the movement for Italian unification: hardly anyone who worked for the Risorgimento had not at one time been his supporter; the idealism of this movement was essentially of his inspiration.

Vicenzo Gioberti was very different in character and approach. In 1833 as a young priest he had been forced to leave his native Piedmont because of his part in an army conspiracy led by Mazzini. He had been court theologian to the crown prince Carlo Alberto at Turin and was highly regarded as a professor of philosophy. He spent some months in prison, then went to Paris and in his years of exile, between 1834 and 1845, he became interested in contemporary philosophy, having earlier studied Malebranche, Spinoza and Giordano Bruno. He was a convert to what he himself defined as ontologism, and like his own fellow countryman, Antonio Rosmini, or the German philosophers Hermes and Günther, he sought to reconcile Catholic belief with modern philosophical thought. According to his system, based on Kant, the human intellect acts in theory and practice on account of its awareness of God and material things which are with God. This awareness emerges in the unfolding of moral consciousness and in this unfolding is realised the divine essence by means of the human spirit. 'Being creates existence and existence returns to being. The mystical moment of the awareness of God is experienced rationally and immanently.' Later he opposed Rosmini who, so as not to offend against orthodox Catholic thinking, based the whole structure of the human intellect upon the categories of being, with the proviso that this merely

supposed being was distinct from real being, which is God. Certain aspects of Gioberti's philosophy, strongly influenced by Hegel and Plato, came close to a mystical pantheism and thus facilitated the condemnation of some of his writings in 1849. In 1847 he provoked the hostility of the Jesuits with his *Il Gesuita Moderno*. When his political plans foundered in 1849, it was the Jesuits who got this book placed on the Index, and when, in 1851, Gioberti expressed his disappointment over the reactionary course of the papacy in *Del Rinnovamento Civile d'Italia,* this book was condemned together with his other philosophical writings. As with Rosmini, whose role in Italian philosophy can be compared to that of Kant in Germany, Gioberti's real significance lies in his work for Italian unification. In 1843, he published his *Primato Morale e Civile degli Italiani* in which he developed his ideas for an Italian confederation under the presidency of the pope. Austria was to be excluded from this renewed Italy which would have Piedmont instead as its military protector. Also excluded would be the Jesuits, whom Gioberti rightly regarded as being mainly responsible for the fatal course of events under Gregory XVI. In almost ecstatic language he hailed Pius IX as the great liberal pope of the future and the liberator of Italy. These ideas which he developed during his exile in Brussels became widely popular. His philosophical and political ideas were discussed in France. For a time the nuncio in Brussels, Vincenzo Gioacchino Pecci, later Leo XIII, was much impressed by his personality. While for Mazzini revolution and subversion were the pre-conditions of Italian national renewal, Gioberti's *neo-guelfismo* sought to satisfy Italian hopes with a moderate programme of liberal reform based on existing conditions. A confederation of constitutional monarchies seemed to him the only possible solution and he had little confidence in a national renewal in Mazzini's sense, or indeed in revolutionary changes. All his plans presupposed, however, a papacy committed to new ideas. It was in this respect that Gioberti agreed with Lamennais, with whom he had otherwise little in common.

Another scholar who advocated an Italian confederation under the guardianship of both the House of Savoy and the pope was the historian Cesare Balbo, later Prime Minister of Piedmont and author of *Speranza d'Italia* (1844). Everything seemed to depend on the next occupant of the Chair of Peter.

The liberalism of Pius IX 1846-8

The death of Gregory XVI in 1846 was thus an event eagerly awaited by many. 'Reactionary, stubborn and inert,' wrote the Italian historian Adolfo Omodeo, 'opposed to every sort of innovation, even to the building of railways, Gregory XVI died after sixteen years of bad government, leaving a difficult heritage to his successor'. Even Cesare Cantu, who sympathised with the papacy, wrote in 1854:

He knew nothing of constitutions, budgets, and other wondrous inventions remote from theology and the kingdom of God, so that he left everything to his ministers and to circumstances. They were responsible for the fact that the reforms promised in 1831 had merely bad effects or none at all. The administration of justice was not only corrupt but constantly exposed to the arbitrary judgments of the courts of appeal. Graft and corruption, the old bane of Rome, intrigues, the arbitrary rule of powerful men and of papal officials grew beyond all bounds.

Rosmini expressed the general feeling when he wrote:

All Italians demand the unity of Italy and there is no one whose heart it does not cause to beat faster. It would therefore be vain to try to prove the usefulness or the necessity of this unity. Where all are agreed there can be no question.

Not even the conclave of 1846 could escape this conclusion, and from the beginning it was marked by the feeling that change could no longer be delayed. Violent objections were raised to Lambruschini, the candidate of the reactionaries, whom the aged cardinal-deacon Mattei even described as *Papa del diavolo*. The election of Giovanni Maria Mastai-Ferretti, of whom Gregory XVI had said disparagingly that in his house even the cats were liberals, was tantamount to a political programme. Mastai, however, was a compromise candidate. The real liberal candidate was cardinal Feltrinelli, but he was committed to reform to such an extent that the unknown Mastai was preferred even by Feltrinelli supporters.

The new Pius was no liberal in any real sense. Frail in health, conspicuously vain and weak though devout, he had familiarised himself with the ideas of Rosmini and Gioberti, but lacked the imagination to put them into practice. He had no plan of his own in which the hopes of liberals and nationalists might be related to the rights of the papacy. Pius IX was full of indignation about his predecessor's regime and wanted to redress past injustice. He began his reign with a general amnesty which enabled many of those who had clearer but also more radical ideas about the Italian future to return to Rome.

His election raised such high hopes also among the revolutionaries that an already well-prepared rising was called off. The pope allowed himself to be carried along by the general rejoicing, but he lacked confidence in handling the highly suspicious curia which with characteristic scorn called him *Pio Nonno*, a pun linking his Italian title *Pio Nono* (Pius IX) with a pious old grandfather (*nonno*). He wavered like a reed in the wind, could not keep the initiative, sought approval where he could and finally got himself hopelessly entangled. He saw himself as the pope of Gioberti's expectation, allowed himself to be fêted as such, but thereby provoked the suspicions of Austria and became identified with a movement of which he himself rejected the ultimate aims. He consented to a ministry with lay participation, to a privy council, he accepted a certain degree of freedom of the press and the setting up of a civil guard. In November 1847 he made an important move towards Italian unification by concluding a customs union with Piedmont and Tuscany. Gioberti's programme seemed almost fulfilled. But the reforms of the liberal pope foundered on the incompatibility, which Gioberti had refused to acknowledge, between a confederation of princes and of those representing the revolutionary aims of the nationalist movement. While Pius believed that he was contributing to the political realisation of Gioberti's ideas, but was actually too weak to carry out internal religious reforms against the curia, the radicals united in order to test their utopian ideas. They accelerated the advance of democracy and on 16 March 1848 this resulted in a new constitution in the Papal States. But now it became evident that hardly any common ground existed between the ideas of Pius IX

Map of Italy showing the progress of Italian unification: a movement which was closely linked with the final abolition of the Papal States.

FRANCE

AUSTRIA-HUNGARY

SWITZERLAND

Solferino (defeat of Austrians) 1859

Custozza (defeat of Italian troops) 1866

LOMBARDY

VENETIA

Magenta (defeat of Austrians) 1859

● Milan

Verona

● Venice

● Trieste

● Fiume

Turin ●

PIEDMONT

PARMA

OTTOMAN EMPIRE

Genoa ●

MODENA

ROMAGNA

SAN MARINO (Independent Republic)

DALMATIA

KINGDOM

● Florence
Capital of Italy 1864-1871

MARCHES

✗ Castelfidardo 1860

OF

TUSCANY

PAPAL STATES

ELBA

UMBRIA

Mentana Garibaldi defeated by the French 3 November 1867

CORSICA (French)

THE PATRIMONY

R. Tiber

✗

(PIEDMONT)

Rome
Entered by Italians 1870
Made Italian Capital 1871

Gaeta 1861 (Pius IX in exile 1848-50)

✗

BENEVENTO (Papal to 1860)

● Naples
Entered by Garibaldi 7th September 1860

SARDINIA

SARDINIA

NAPLES

KINGDOM OF THE TWO SICILIES

✗ Aspromonte
Garibaldi captured 29th August 1862

● Palermo
Entered by Garibaldi 6th June 1860

SICILY

Seizure of the Quirinal, then the seat of papal government,
by the insurgent Roman crowd on 24 November 1848.
Pius IX fled to Gaeta and the Roman Republic was proclaimed.

and those of the democrats. In the new constitution the two chambers
were placed under the consistory of cardinals; parliament was given
no control over ecclesiastical questions, over financial affairs insofar
as they concerned the church as a universal institution, and over
the larger part of foreign affairs. The powers of this parliament
were limited to an extent that might seem to reduce it to utter in-
significance. But with the transfer of governmental functions to

secular hands, an essential part of the revolutionary demands was nevertheless fulfilled, and further constitutional developments would undoubtedly have been possible on this basis.

Pius IX in exile 1848-50

What decided matters in Rome was the new revolutionary wave from France. When the revolutionary turmoil overwhelmed Austria and the multi-national empire was close to disintegration, Pius, urged on by fanatical crowds, allowed himself to be drawn into preparations for a war of liberation to be waged jointly by all the Italian states. Austrian resistance, however, quickly hardened and brought him to his senses. In his address to the cardinals on 29 April 1848, which marks the turning point of his pontificate, he renounced the use of armed force and declared his neutrality. Now the mood changed dramatically. Pius was accused of having betrayed the patriotic cause. His cabinet, including cardinal Antonelli, later to be secretary of state, but at this time still leading the liberal cardinals, joined the war against the pope's will. Utterly lost, Pius tried to persuade the Austrians to give up their Italian provinces voluntarily. He himself held out in Rome for another six months, making all kinds of promises, trying to adopt a conservative policy and getting himself into even deeper trouble. In September he appointed the competent and energetic Pellegrino Rossi as Prime Minister, but when Rossi was assassinated on 15 November, the revolt could no longer be contained. On 24 November Pius IX escaped to Gaeta, which was Neapolitan territory, in the carriage of the Bavarian ambassador. Before leaving he threatened with ecclesiastical penalties all those participating in democratic institutions in Rome or in the government. But now the radicals were masters in their own house. Mazzini and Garibaldi took over the leadership. At Gaeta Pius felt as though he had escaped from a volcano. It was not diffi-

Picture of a meeting that never took place:
Pius IX, Victor Emmanuel II, first king of all Italy,
and Garibaldi, as seen by an anonymous artist.
A light-hearted expression of the hopes of many
Italians wishing to reconcile love for their country
with loyalty to the Church.

cult for members of the curial party to convince him that what had happened was but the foreseeable outcome of an alliance with the liberals, which Pius now came to see in the same way as his predecessors. Since he had never seriously studied liberal ideas, he was quite unable to distinguish between justified demands and the excesses of mob rule, and to realise the benefits which the papacy could have derived from these ideas. His liberalism was a whim which he indulged because it made him popular and won him support among the people. To a man of his sensitive and pastoral outlook, this mattered more than anything else. Events seemed to prove to him that one could not govern with kindness, and also (as he had been told ad nauseam) that liberalism was equivalent to rebellion and hostility to religion, and that the movement for Italian national unification was a form of idolatry. The events in Rome after his flight to Gaeta seemed an ominous confirmation of this. In the pope's view a distinction between moderate liberals and revolutionaries was no longer possible. Lambruschini's influence became dominant at Gaeta and proved a much needed support for the suffering pope in his two years of exile. Gaeta was the beginning of the tragedy of Catholic liberalism anticipated by Lamennais under Gregory XVI. 'The liberal Catholics took flight into a formula that was never mentioned but always applied, that liberalism was not against religion, but only against the temporal interests of the church, which cannot and ought not to be mixed up with those of religion.'[2] Having been the national hope of Catholic Italy at the beginning of the century, the papacy lost all the support it had acquired. Italians accepted the termination of clerical government with indifference; the rigid *non possumus* with which cardinal secretary of state Antonelli answered all attempts at compromise found no echo among his compatriots.

Pius IX, and to an even greater degree his secretary of state, made the great mistake to which conservatives are often prone: they

thought that they could maintain their position by disregarding all the circumstances that made it no longer tenable. When Gioberti became Prime Minister of Piedmont on 16 December 1848, he offered the pope Piedmontese assistance because he rightly feared that a renewed papal appeal for foreign troops would lead to an irreparable breach between the papacy and the movement for Italian independence. The offer was brusquely refused; the pope wanted nothing more to do with this false prophet, as he now thought of him, although only in the spring of that year he had cordially received him in audience. Rosmini too, whom Gioberti had sent as special envoy to Pius, lost what influence he formerly had. As late as 1847 the pope wanted to make Rosmini a cardinal, but by 1848 Rosmini's position had been undermined to such an extent by his rival Antonelli that some of his writings were placed on the Index.

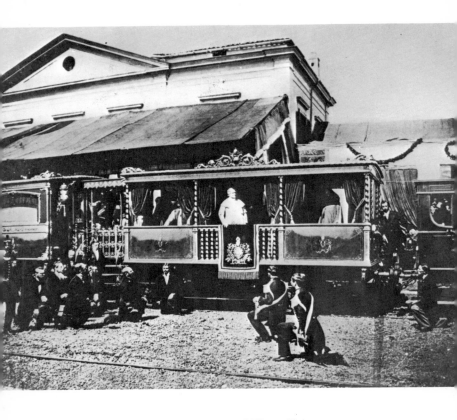

The Syllabus and the defeat of liberalism

The breach between Pius IX and *neo-guelfismo* was now complete.
Having returned to Rome in 1850 under the protection of the
French army, Pius IX was able to maintain himself in the Papal
States only with the support of French bayonets and foreign mer-
cenaries. Reaction was elevated to a political principle; constitutional democracies were declared irreconcilable with the papacy.
Quite apart from its attitude towards religion, liberalism in all its
forms became suspect and was fought against and condemned. If
Antonelli had had his way, the temporal power of the papacy would
have been declared a dogma of the church, although the government
of the Papal States (and through it the prestige of the papacy) was

Pius IX on the blessing platform of the first
papal train at Velletri in 1863.

87

undermined by the deplorable conditions for which Antonelli was mainly responsible more than by anything else. Even during the First Vatican Council there were attempts to make the temporal power of the papacy an article of Catholic belief.

With that blindness with which, it is said, God strikes those whose downfall he intends, the papacy tried to stop a tide that could not be held back. Gioberti too, who had long defended the existence of the Papal States, was now convinced that they must disappear in the church's own best interests. In retaliation his writings were placed on the Index. Those who dared criticise the government in the Papal States were considered to be enemies of the church; among them were Döllinger, Lacordaire and that group of Italian priests who, in 1863, petitioned the pope to reconcile himself with the aims of the nation and renounce his secular powers.

Before the Italian troops finally occupied Rome on 20 September 1870, the Italian policy of Pius IX was laid down in two declarations which had great importance for the papacy's future relationship with the modern world. After 1860 all that remained of the Papal States was the *Patrimonium Petri* and it was only a question of time before this area too would be absorbed by the new Italian kingdom. Napoleon III, the protector both of Italian independence and the pope, was pressed again and again by Cavour to leave the solution of the Roman question to the Italians. Cavour had prepared various memoranda in which, on the basis of the principle of a free church in a free state, he outlined the legal position and the freedom of the papacy within the Italian kingdom. On 15 September 1854 an agreement was reached between Piedmont and Napoleon III in which the vaccillating Emperor undertook to withdraw his troops within two years. Understandably Pius was deeply angered when he heard of this. In December 1864 he replied with the encyclical *Quanta cura,* a passionate condemnation of rationalism, Gallicanism, liberalism and communism. Also condemned was the theological

Pius IX being offered the keys of Rome
on 12 April 1850 after his triumphal
return to Rome from exile in Gaeta.

doctrine known as naturalism. This denied the existence of a transcendental God and of supernatural acts, and would not accept the need of revelation and the church. Appended was the notorious *Syllabus errorum*, a collection of eighty statements, condemning the errors of the age. They were extracted from former encyclicals, consistorial addresses and apostolic letters of the pope, and divided into ten sections:

1 pantheism, naturalism and absolute rationalism;
2 moderate rationalism;
3 indifferentism;
4 socialism, communism, secret societies, bible societies and liberal clerical associations;
5 errors concerning the church and her rights;
6 errors concerning the state and its relations with the church;
7 errors concerning natural and Christian morality;
8 errors concerning Christian marriage;
9 errors concerning the temporal rule of the pope;
10 errors relating to modern liberalism.

From a Catholic point of view there was some justification for the Syllabus, but some sections, especially 4, 5, 6, 9 and 10, were depressing reading for many Catholics, even in those days. It has been pointed out that the Syllabus carried the signature not of Pius, but only of Antonelli, and that it must be related to the writings which it quotes and condemns. From the outset, however, the Syllabus was included among the infallible papal pronouncements, not only by opponents of the church but also by many Catholic theologians and members of the curia. Pius never protested against this nor against the view that his condemnation was not a matter compelling obedient acceptance. Both views were maintained by Catholic theologians and Pius did nothing to elucidate a document so liable to misinterpretation. On the contrary, he added to the confusion by commending *La Convention du 15 septembre et*

l'Encyclique du 8 décembre by the bishop of Orleans, Dupanloup, Montalembert's friend and collaborator. Dupanloup had emphasised the time-bound character and Italian setting of the Syllabus and denied that it implied a condemnation of Catholic participation in liberal governments. At the same time, however, Pius praised *L'Illusion libérale* (1865) by Louis Veuillot, a brilliant French journalist, editor of *L'Univers* and staunch supporter of Napoleon III, yet Veuillot had demanded the literal interpretation of the Syllabus.

But however it is interpreted, the Syllabus goes a good deal further than the notorious *Mirari vos* and constitutes the papacy's clearest rejection of the times up to this point. Taken together with the decisions of the First Vatican Council, it involved the papacy

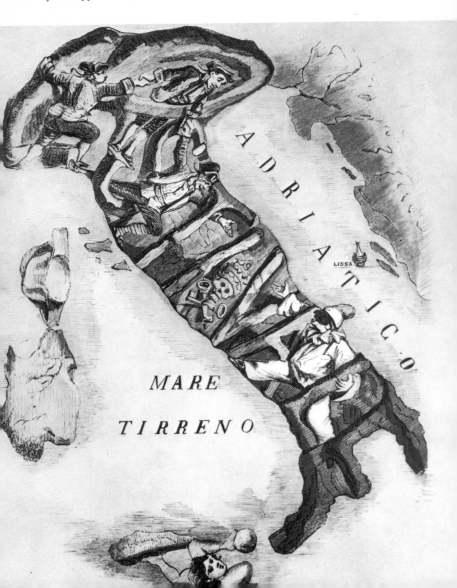

Lo Stivale, ('The Boot'), illustrating the Italian struggle
for independence in 1866. The figures represent Venice,
Piedmont and Tuscany striving to join the South, but papal Rome
bars the way. This cartoon by Martelli is inspired by a famous
satirical poem on the history of Italy, *Lo Stivale*
by Giuseppe Giusti, one of the poets of the Risorgimento.

The surrender of the papal troops on
the battlements of Rome on 20 September
1870 after the famous breach of
the gates of Porta Pia, through which
the Italian troops entered Rome.
A column now commemorates the event.

in a grave crisis, endangering its apostolic mission and lowering it
to the status of a world-despising sect.

Like the Syllabus, the decree *Non expedit* of 29 February 1868,
which forbade Italians to take part in elections, can be explained
only against the Italian background. It was less the overthrow of the
Papal States, as is often suggested, than the victory over Garibaldi
at Mentana on 3 November 1867, which caused this declaration
that for years poisoned relations with parliamentary democracy.

When Rome was occupied by Italian troops on 20 September 1870
the pope anathematised the conquerors. It was the last time that this
traditional condemnation was imposed for a political issue. Yet in
the referendum of 20 October 1870 only 1507 of the 167,548 who
were entitled to vote decided against the union of the Papal States
with the kingdom of Italy. By their own choice Pius IX and his
successors condemned themselves to be prisoners in the Vatican
until 1929. The Piedmontese occupation troops were confronted
by chaotic conditions in the papal administration. It fell to them to

disband the Jewish ghetto in Rome, the last one in Europe. A direct line leads from *Mirari vos* to the events of 20 September 1870. The curia's anti-liberal and reactionary policy and its antagonism to the times was bound to produce political disaster.

It soon became evident that the universal character of the papacy and its international mission did not depend on small territorial possessions. Far from impeding the rise of the papacy to a position of world influence, this was indeed facilitated and promoted by the abolition of its temporal power.

5 The victory of neo-scholasticism

The school of neo-scholasticism was founded in Naples at the beginning of the eighteen thirties by the Jesuits, Luigi Taparelli d'Azeglio and Matteo Liberator. Liberatore's *Institutiones Philosophicae* (1840), was the first modern synthesis of Thomist philosophy. In 1850 both men founded *La Civiltà Cattolica,* the Jesuit review that was soon to gain considerable influence in Rome. However, in spite of the òfficial support that neo-scholasticism and Thomism received under Gregory XVI and Pius IX, they reached their dominant influence in Catholic theology only under Leo XIII.

The new theology in Germany

Neo-scholasticism soon flourished in Rome, where all attempts at reconciling modern philosophy with Catholicism met with suspicion. Above all, these attempts were made in Germany by eminent Protestant divines such as Friedrich Schleiermacher, Johann August Neander, Ferdinand Christian Bauer and Adolf von Harless. After the dissolution of the Catholic universities at the time of the secularisation, the founding of joint Catholic-Protestant theological faculties in the universities of Tübingen, Bonn, Breslau and Giessen was a new feature in German academic life. They favoured an intellectual exchange unthinkable in former centuries, which was to prove highly beneficial to German Catholic theology and raise it to a leading position within the Catholic church in the nineteenth century. These theological faculties soon became highly suspect in Rome, where even the university training of theologians in purely Catholic faculties such as existed in Munich, was opposed. Rome wanted to protect Catholic theologians from the dangerous contamination of non-Catholics or the enemies of the church, and has persisted in this attitude, at considerable cost, up to the present day. The Tübingen school in particular achieved eminence in Catholic theology. Its founder, Johann Sebastian Drey, and Johann Adam

Möhler were among the most distinguished Catholic theologians of their time. Under the leadership of Johann Baptist von Hirscher and Karl Joseph von Hefele, who later became Bishop of Rottenburg, the Tübingen school exerted a decisive influence on Catholic theology and its attempts to come to terms with modern scholarship. Its influence diminished only after the proclamation of the dogma of papal infallibility against which Hefele above all had fought in vain. Of similar importance was the Munich school of Joseph Görres, with Ignaz Döllinger, perhaps the greatest church historian of the nineteenth century, among its followers.

Neo-scholasticism found its first German home in Mainz where Johann Baptist Heinrich and Franz Christoph Moufang followed the teaching of Franz Jacob Clemens, a professor from Münster and a bitter opponent of Anton Günther, whose attempt to provide a natural and nationalist explanation of the Catholic dogmas on the lines of German idealism was conemned in Rome. The German conservative theologians agreed with the Roman objections to the university training of priests, and the opening of the Mainz seminary on 1 May 1851 by Von Ketteler, who later became a famous bishop and pioneer in the social field, was something of a challenge. A Catholic theological faculty survived at Giessen until 1859, when its professor died. Matthias Scheeben (1835-88), the greatest of the German neo-scholastics, taught at the Cologne seminary, but his influence was not felt until after the Vatican Council of 1870. It was probably due to the more enclosed teaching in seminaries that even a man like Scheeben had few followers, while the theological faculties, Tübingen in particular, were remarkable for the continuity of their teaching and for their endeavours to interpret revelation according to changing human circumstances. The theological faculties rather than the seminaries became a testing ground for new ideas. From 1859-90 Heinrich and Moufang edited the review, *Katholik*, which, founded in 1821, soon became the leading German organ of neo-scholasticism, a model also for the Roman *La Civiltà Cattolica*. Heinrich exerted a considerable influence on Ketteler and his social writings and measures; both Heinrich and Moufang were violent opponents of the new theology. They believed that the German universities had ceased to be Christian, that Catholic theology lacked proper bases although these had long existed unrecognised in the philosophy of Aquinas as taught in Rome. Most of the denunciations in Rome of the representatives of the new theology came from among the German neo-scholastics.

The new theology condemned by Rome

The attempts to reconcile modern philosophy and theology were checked in the early 1830s. David Friedrich Strauss caused a sensation in 1835 with his book *Das Leben Jesu* ('The Life of Jesus'), based on the new methods of source criticism, in which he made a sharp distinction between the historical and the mythological Jesus. It was a turning point for evangelical theology. Conservative

Catholic theologians regarded this book as dangerous proof of what happened when the new scientific methods were applied to theology. Their rejection of these methods endangered the position of Catholic theology in the universities. A serious conflict broke out at Bonn where Georg Hermes taught theology, and ended in 1835 with the condemnation of the schools founded by him, called Hermesianism. Hermes and his followers had gone too far in trying to integrate the philosophy of Kant with Catholic doctrine; Rome certainly had grounds for their condemnation but it was the German elements rather than the Roman which were responsible for the witch hunt that ensued.

Hermes was repeatedly denounced in Rome by, among others, the zealous archbishop of Cologne, Droste-Vischering, before being summarily condemned. No reasons were given for a sentence that was later shown to have been based on unreliable evidence. But his condemnation merely increased his fame. His speculative theology and his methodological approach have been a formative influence for many later theologians, Scheeben among them.

The case of Franz von Baader was handled a little more skilfully. Baader, one of the most original Catholic philosophers in nineteenth-century Germany, was not driven out of the church although he made no secret of his opposition to Rome and rejected the papal primacy. The Strasbourg theologian Louis Eugène Marie Bautain, a leading opponent of scholasticism, owed it to Möhler's intervention that he was saved from a breach with Rome, but he had nevertheless to qualify his teachings. In *La Philosophie du Christianisme* (1835), Bautain had advocated the traditionalistic thesis of common sense as the only source of scientific knowledge.

Anton Günther was the third eminent Catholic scholar after Lamennais and Hermes to be denounced and condemned. For forty years he had tried to raise the scholastic level of Catholic theology. However, his condemnation, unlike that of Lamennais and Hermes, was preceded by a thorough investigation in Rome, in which his supporters were also given a chance to be heard. His downfall was caused by his intemperate attacks on neo-scholasticism, and this doctrine was given a first official papal blessing on the occasion of his condemnation in 1857.

The condemnation of ontologism between 1861 and 1866 caused a similar sensation in France to that of Günther's in Germany. During his exile in Brussels Gioberti had coined the term for the philosophical theory according to which God is known through an intuitive idea of reason as the primal image of all ideas and as the metaphysical, eternal, unalterable essence of creation. At the time of Gioberti's condemnation, ontologism was the dominant teaching at the Sorbonne among French Dominicans, Benedictines and Jesuits. It would oversimplify matters to see these 'heresies' – and I have only mentioned the more important ones – as expressions of particular national modes of thought, Güntherianism and the Tübingen school bearing the marks of Germany, and ontologism those of France. But these national traits cannot be denied; they certainly had as much influence in Rome as neo-scholasticism in having their opponents condemned. In most cases up to 1870 these condemnations had some justification, but the Roman authorities undoubtedly went out of their way to procure incriminating evidence. The procedure is best exemplified by the treatment of Antonio Rosmini. For many years he was a trusted adviser of Gregory XVI and Pius IX. Then suddenly in 1849 two of his political works were placed on the Index, and his opponents tried to get his philosophical doctrine condemned as well. An investigation of these writings, ordered by Pius IX, ended with them being officially declared free from error in 1854. But in 1887, twenty-two years after his death, he was again condemned on the strength of forged evidence. Statements from his writings were taken out of their context and strung together in such a way as to produce heretical doctrines.

Left John Emerich Edward Dalberg-Acton, 1st Baron (1834–1902). As owner and co-editor with Newman and Richard Simpson, Acton edited the 'Rambler', 'Home and Foreign Review', 'North British Review'. This remarkable experiment in English liberal Catholic journalism ended, however, before the 1864 Syllabus could put an official stop to it. He opposed the proclamation of papal infallibility on historical grounds but, like Newman and unlike Döllinger, he accepted

The growing Roman belief that any dealing with contemporary philosophy was devil's work was accompanied by efforts within the curia to get neo-scholasticism recognised as the sole road to Catholic truth. This trend affected John Henry Newman in England no less than Döllinger in Germany, who, at the Munich Congress of German Catholic scholars in 1863, attempted to heal the rift with the neo-scholastics. In his speech, however, he castigated the scholastics for serving up arguments that had already failed at the time of the reformation. Döllinger compared Roman neo-scholasticism with German theological thinking, which, he declared rather tactlessly, used guns for the defence of the faith, while the Romans were still fighting with bows and arrows. This was enough to make him completely unacceptable to the Roman authorities. The final clash came with the struggle over the dogma of papal infallibility, advocated most fervently by the neo-scholastics. The defeat of the German and French bishops and theologians who opposed the dogma also decided the hegemony of neo-scholasticism in Rome.

the Vatican Council's definition. He was the first Catholic since the Reformation to hold the Regius Chair of Modern History at Cambridge and edited the 'Cambridge Modern History'. He has become famous for a number of historical *obiter dicta*, such as 'Power tends to corrupt, absolute power corrupts absolutely ... great men are almost invariably bad men'.
Right John Henry Newman at the time of the Vatican Council.

Papal infallibility: the triumph of the curia

Immediately after the publication of the Syllabus on 8 December 1864, Pius IX told the cardinals in strictest secrecy of his intention to call a general Council. He had already entertained this idea while he was at Gaeta. In 1854 two hundred bishops from all over the world had been invited to Rome for discussions on the proposed dogma of the Immmaculate Conception. They gave their consent to the examination and promulgation of the dogma. When over five hundred bishops came to Rome in June 1867 to celebrate the eighteen hundredth anniversary of the martyrdom of St Peter, Pius used the occasion for announcing the Council. The bull of invitation went out on 29 June 1868. Opinions were divided about the forthcoming Council, but an article published in the Jesuit review, *La Civiltà Cattolica* on 6 February 1869 caused grave concern to many. It stated that the Council would define by general acclamation the papal teaching contained in the Syllabus as well as papal infallibility.

It was a particularly clumsy procedure to link the Syllabus with

infallibility, since it made the latter doctrine appear to be a pro-
vocative measure directed in the same way against the errors of the
times. The protagonists of extreme ultramontanism and the curia
added to this impression by their fanatical behaviour. Döllinger
was among those who opposed these zealots. His five *Letters of
Quirinus* which he published in the *Augsburger Allgemeine Zeitung*
caused a sensation far beyond Germany. In England, Döllinger
had a loyal ally in his former pupil Sir John (later Lord) Acton,
who propagated the views of his German mentor in the learned
Catholic reviews the *Rambler* and *Home and Foreign Review*,
edited by Acton and Newman. Fearing the political consequence of
papal infallibility, Döllinger tried to mobilise the Bavarian cabinet,
which consulted other governments, but without effect.

Pius IX opened the Council on 8 December 1869. In solemn procession 774 of the 1084 Council Fathers entitled to attend entered

Ceremonial entry of the seven
hundred and seventy-four Council
Fathers into the right arm of
the transept of St Peter's,
where the First Vatican Council
opened on 8 February 1869.

101

and took up their places in the right transept of St Peter's. The Council agenda was drawn up by the pope and hardly permitted a full debate; he reserved all decisions to himself. Opposition was curbed by limiting the duration of speeches. All protests were in vain; indeed, Pius reacted to them with petulance. Through skilful manipulations those who opposed infallibility among the German, Italian, French and American bishops were excluded from the commission which made the final decisions and had to express their views in the public sessions. A full debate in which these objections could have been considered was prevented. On 24 April 1870 the dogmatic constitution on the Catholic faith was proclaimed in which, once again, Hermesianism, Güntherianism, ontologism and Traditionalism were condemned. Of these, only Traditionalism had until then not been anathematised although some French synods had already condemned it. The doctrine denied that man by himself is capable of attaining truth but held that all truth is derived from divine revelation and its traditions, or, as Lamennais held, from general reason as revealed in the common consent of mankind.

The real climax of the Council came with the debate on infallibility. Having been rejected by the Council of Constance and Basle, this issue had not been clearly resolved by the Council of Trent. Gallicanism, Febronianism, Josephinism and Jansenism were as fervently against papal infallibility as the Roman authorities were in favour of it. In the nineteenth century the demand for this dogma came especially from the Traditionalists, inspired by Lamennais, and from the curia and the Italian Jesuits. Pius IX finally submitted the text of the dogma on 6 March 1870. On 29 April all other debates were interrupted in order to give precedence to this dogma, contrary to the wishes of its opponents. The opposition party which comprised 136 Council Fathers expressed its objections in speeches and writings. Hefele (of Rottenburg) dealt with the historical objections, Rauscher (of Vienna) spoke on the dogmatic and Ketteler

Solemn proclamation of the dogma of papal infallibility in St Peter's on 18 July 1870. It was also a gesture of defiance to the Italian troops closing in on Rome. Rome was occupied on 20 September and on 20 October Pius IX adjourned the Council *sine die*. As a result, many vital church problems, in particular the power of the bishops in relation to that of the pope, had to wait for a settlement until the Second Vatican Council in 1962.

(of Mainz) on the practical implications. The debate was suddenly broken off on 13 June; about a hundred Council Fathers protested in vain to the pope. Pius felt that he was under personal attack as he had himself frequently intervened in the debate by citing the conflicting opinions of theologians. The first ballot produced 451 *placet* or yea, 88 *non placet* or nay and 62 *placet iuxta modum,* yea subject to certain amendments. This result seemed so favourable to the opponents of infallibility that they offered to relent if some of their objections were met. But Pius rejected all the proposed modifications. On 17 July the minority, in accordance with a proposal by Hefele, was prepared to refuse submission and to vote against the dogma in public session. But in order to avoid this scandal, the 88 bishops finally decided to leave Rome before the Council made its momentous decision.

On 18 June 1870 the dogma of papal infallibility was accepted by 535 votes for and two against. By the light of a taper, while a thunderstorm raged over the Eternal City, Pius read the Constitution in a voice that was hardly audible. The decisive passage reads:

That the Roman Pontiff, when he speaks *ex cathedra,* that is, when, in discharge of the office of pastor and teacher of Christians, by virtue of his supreme apostolic authority, he defines a doctrine regarding faith or morals to be held by the universal church, is by the divine assistance promised to him in Blessed Peter possessed of that infallibility with which the Divine Redeemer willed that His church should be endowed in defining doctrine regarding faith or morals; and that therefore, such definitions of the Roman Pontiff are of themselves, and not from the consent of the church, irrevocable.

On the following day, 19 July, the Franco-Prussian war broke out and prevented the resumption of the Council, so that important questions such as the doctrine of the church as a whole, including the position of bishops, in relation to the infallible pope could not be dealt with.

The results of the dogma

The dogma of papal infallibility affected the internal situation of the church in two ways. In the first place the position of bishops and their relation to the pope were transformed by papal absolutism. The bishops lost their independence and became officials of the pope. This development had been anticipated in the concordats concluded since 1814, which had limited the scope of episcopal powers in favour of direct agreements between governments and pope. It signalled the final defeat of the centripetal powers which the bishops had assumed in the seventeenth and eighteenth centuries and the final victory of Roman centralism. In the second place, the dominant position of the pope in the teaching office of the church assured the virtual victory of neo-scholasticism and Thomism, although these had no actual connection with the teaching office. Roman decisions were of course accepted without opposition throughout the Catholic church even before 1870, but now Rome became the sole source of theological decisions as well, and to such an extent that no new theological trends were possible without

Vatican approval. Hitherto an absence of condemnation implied approval, now approval had to be explicitly sought. The position of the curia was enhanced beyond all measure.

Roman centralisation, which enabled the machinery of the curia to assume dominance, also affected secular absolutism. The pope was now seen as the representative of the divinely-inspired papacy, with the curia acting as its real and timeless agent. Decisions which were issued on behalf of the pope came anonymously from the curia. The marked conservative trend which was supported by Gregory xvi and Pius ix, and was to all appearances confirmed by the events of the years 1846-8, now came to affect theology, since with the dissolution of the Papal States the curia was deprived of any political outlet. All theological experiment was discouraged. The world was expected to accept the thesis that the truths of the Catholic church could only be taught in a form which was timeless and was removed from actual realities.

What was now important was the relationship which Catholics outside Italy formed with Rome. Italians were accustomed to bearing the political decisions of the pope like a cross especially imposed upon them, but for them it was easier since basically they agreed with the theological decisions. Indeed, the more reactionary ecclesiastical government became in the church's own narrow territory, the easier it was to ignore her voice in temporal matters. A similar trend now developed among Catholics in other countries.

6 International relations 1831-78

In 1830-1 the papacy because of its apparent acceptance of the *Zeitgeist* was suspected of leading a conspiracy against the status quo, yet forty years later it was exposed to similar accusations through its very hostility to the times.

Lamennais had gone to Rome in 1830-1 to beg the papacy to lead the revolution. The national risings in Belgium, Ireland, Poland and south America had a definite Catholic ring. To Metternich in 1830-1 Catholicism seemed almost a fifth column. But forty years later, in 1871, the French Prime Minister observed that since the dissolution of the Papal States, Catholicism had become the 'Black International', a menace no less dangerous than the Red International of socialism.

There was, however, a decisive difference, and it marks the shift of the papacy's position from the centre of world affairs to the periphery. The alliance between pope and Catholics to which the French Revolution had given birth, and the resulting papal hegemony in the Catholic world had not had the effect of linking the papacy more closely with contemporary trends, but rather was used by it to keep such ideas away from Rome. Throughout the nineteenth and twentieth centuries the relationship between faithful and papacy was never other than that between subject and sovereign. This was the basis of the papacy's independence, allowing it to become a valuable ally of the forces of restoration in 1831, and a strong counter-weight to constitutionalism and capitalism after 1870. Paradoxical though it may sound, the very lack of freedom of the Catholic church in various countries helped to confirm the papacy's freedom and its indisputable right of leadership. It managed both to restrain its former national rivals, the bishops, and to provide support for Catholics in conflict with their governments which the latter found difficult to contest. In these four decades we can note two phases in the relations between papacy and governments. In the first individual governments or intellectual movements

Below Cardinal Acton, uncle of the historian Sir John (later Baron) Acton, acting as interpreter between Gregory XVI and Tsar Nicholas I in a discussion on the Polish question. *Right* Polish Catholics attending a service in a churchyard during the rising of 1863 in which Catholics took a leading part.

tried to use the papacy for their own ends. In the second the interests of Catholics were handled by the papacy for its own ends.

The hopes of Catholic countries longing for independence were shattered by Gregory XVI. His unconditional acceptance of the existing order helped to seal the fate of the Irish and Polish struggle for freedom. Belgium was a special case; Lamennais' concept of a free church in a free state was there applied in practice and favoured the nationalist cause. But Belgian independence was decided less by the approval of the church than by the policy of the great powers; Gregory himself would rather have supported the restoration of Protestant Orange rule. But finally he too was compelled, much against his will, to recognise the separation of church and state in Belgium (and also in the United States) and to tolerate Catholic participation in the political scene. The church had always violently opposed this participation, but nevertheless it had proved its worth by shielding the Catholic church in these countries from the repercussions which the Syllabus and the dogma of papal infallibility had caused elsewhere. No such advantage derived from the refusal of Gregory XVI and Pius IX to support the Polish struggle for independence. The hope of getting the Tsarist Government to agree by way of a counter-deal over Poland to a reunion of the Russian Orthodox Church with Rome proved illusory. The Russian monarchy clung to its pattern of a church wholly subject to the state, and even personal representations failed to change its attitude towards Catholic subjects who had to suffer cruel persecutions.

Attempts to reconcile church and state: 1 France

The questionable nature of the alliance of the papacy and the monarchies was first demonstrated towards the mid-nineteenth century in Germany and France. The settlement reached by concordats and ecclesiastical treaties led to difficulties for Catholics

Charles Comte de Montalembert (1810–70), writer and historian, was the English-born son of a French emigré. He, with Lacordaire (1802–61) and Frederic Ozanam (1815–53) was an enthusiastic follower of Lamennais. Montalembert coined the famous remark, often ascribed to the Duke of Wellington, that the battle of Waterloo was won on the playing fields of Eton.

since these agreements contained no provisions for their political loyalties. Lamennais had already questioned whether governments which merely observed the letter of the concordats could still be regarded as Christian. He also questioned whether the Catholic church should allow herself to be tied to the observance of juridical settlements. It was shown that the commitment to the old order laid down in the concordats and in *Mirari vos* had turned the Catholic population into wholly passive subjects as they were under the *ancien régime*. This was clearly intended by Gregory XVI but, as Lamennais had foreseen, it proved fatal to the church because of the oppressive measures adopted by the French and German governments against her. Thus, after the condemnation of Lamennais, his French supporters, especially Montalembert, sought another road to democracy. Rather than continue to fight for Catholic participation in the state and in society, they tried merely to guard the rights of the Catholic church in a society and state which they accepted as being indifferent, if not hostile, to religion.

The lying-in-state of archbishop Affre.
He was shot on the barricades on 27 June 1848
in an attempt to pacify the contending sides.

Montalembert's actions were based on a sober estimate of what was politically permissible and possible. This caused him occasionally to go too far in his tactics and to apply the very methods of political compromise for which he had criticised his liberal opponents. His *Parti Catholique* founded in 1844 suffered in Rome a fate similar to that of Lamennais. Although it was not banned, its attempt to unify Catholics politically foundered on constant opposition in Rome where no one, least of all Gregory XVI, was well disposed towards the emergence of Catholic political parties.

In the eighteen-thirties a third Catholic attempt to reconcile the ideas of the French Revolution with the church was made in France by Philippe Joseph Benjamin Buchez (1796-1865). His concept of a new kind of Catholic education was based upon what he regarded as the Christian substance of the ideas of 1789. He found widespread support. Originally a follower of Saint-Simon and his 'new Christianity', Buchez was particularly interested in social reform. He is the father of French trade unionism. The Association of Working Men which he founded had the blessing of the French episcopate and, in particular, of the archbishop of Paris, Monsignor Affre. While his association proved successful only for artisans, his general theories made an impact later on French Catholicism concerned with social problems. It is largely due to him that the French Revolution of 1848, unlike that of 1830, was free from anti-Catholic tendencies. In the June rebellion of 1848 archbishop Affre was killed by a stray bullet as he mounted a barricade in an endeavour to establish peace between the workers and the advancing government troops. The Revolution shattered the unity of workers and church and destroyed for a time the relationship between the church and the dismayed middles classes. Eventually, however, a close bond was forged between the French church and the bourgeoisie, initially with the support of Rome, and this became a characteristic feature of France in the second half of the nineteenth century.

2 Germany

In Germany the complete destruction of all the former Catholic institutions produced an alliance with the new restoration regimes that was secured by concordats. Years of pastoral neglect as well as the treatment of Catholics as second-class citizens in the Protestant states undermined the self-confidence of German Catholics. The ideas of Lamennais had not been entirely without response; they were echoed in Franz von Baader's repeated warnings against too close a commitment of the church with the new monarchies, but, on the whole, German Catholics resigned themselves to their position as members of an established church, tolerated but not approved. Matters were made worse by Catholic indifference to social problems and between 1845 and 1848 there was a marked decline in the number of Catholics. Their persecution by the Prussian government, which produced the Cologne church conflict of 1837 and the dispute over the Trier Pilgrimage of 1844, did, however, indirectly promote the renewal of Catholicism. German Catholic emancipation found a brilliant leader in Joseph Görres (1776-1848). The year 1848, a year of revolution, gave rise to many Catholic associations and political parties, which accelerated the process of liberating the church from the fetters of the restoration monarchies.

The emergence after 1830 of Catholic political parties in France, Belgium and Germany seemed in Roman eyes a menacing resurgence of the old middle or 'grey' zone of Christendom. These Catholic parties were set up as defensive movements against governments that disregarded the rights of the church. From the outset, they considered themselves as Catholic pressure groups rather than as parts of a democratic form of government. Catholics were beginning to resist the state with the legal means at their disposal, but they did not attempt, like Lamennais, to bring about a new social order founded on Catholic principles. The democratic system and participation within it were regarded as means to a limited end and no longer as serving an over-riding ideal. There were, indeed, many good Catholic democrats, but Christian democracy did not become the new social order based on Catholicism which the Jansenists, the clergy and bishops of 1789 and Lamennais had envisaged. It remained one among many forces in a pluralist society. But this acceptance by the church of a position of subservience conflicted with three essential principles: her claims to be the sole representative of divine truth in the world, to be 'catholic', that is to say, to represent the whole of mankind, and to keep all nations under the care of the vicar of Christ on earth.

Gregory's alliance of throne and altar, which in practice meant the submission of the church to a monarchy indifferent to religion, was clearly contrary to the nature of the Catholic church. But whether the transformation of the democratic republic into a democratic theocracy, as advocated by Lamennais, could have taken place is another question. Lamennais was right at least in recognising that after 1789 no reconstruction of society that was not based on the freedom of the individual was possible.

The chance to reconstruct society by using the close link between faithful and papacy had certainly been destroyed for a long time to come by *Mirari vos*. Catholics continued to cling to the old social order and were forced to realise that it was the enemies of the church, the hated liberals and socialists, who were shaping the new society from which they had excluded themselves. But the Catholic church's claim to be the sole guardian of truth persisted even though the number of those acknowledging it was steadily decreasing: the withdrawal into a Catholic ghetto was thus unavoidable.

Catholic illusions about the papacy

For a time this conflict was concealed, but it erupted when Gregory XVI took up the cudgels for the state, and, in the dispute between Louis-Philippe and the Jesuits, compelled the latter to give way. Angrily Montalembert commented: 'What does the Holy Father want? Does he want governments and their organs alone to decide matters of religion? Does he want independent Catholics to refrain from using rights, granted by their country's constitution, in order to defend the liberties of the church in political assemblies and in the press?' And bitterly he observed: 'The laity's efforts on behalf of the church have never been encouraged!' It was inconceivable to Montalembert and to Ketteler that Rome could reject democracy outright, that she should consider that any connection with liberalism was inspired by the devil, and that, as her protest against the Austrian constitution of 1867 indicated, all constitutions were anathema to her. Neither the French liberal Catholics nor later the leaders of the German Centre Party understood that what the papacy disliked above all was the position of Catholic parties as mediators between state and church, and that Rome preferred to keep control of diplomatic negotiations at all stages. The papacy looked upon the Catholic political parties as the successors of the hated episcopal power structures of the eighteenth century, and feared an alliance between the state and its Catholic citizens over which Rome would have no control and which would also be against its system of centralisation. This attitude was beyond the comprehension of the ultramontane-minded politicians in France and Germany who, precisely because they regarded themselves as the most loyal sons of the church, cherished illusions about Rome that had no relation to reality. Reporting in the *Correspondant* on his visit to Rome, Frédéric Ozanam wrote in February 1848: 'Having grown old at the deathbed of absolute monarchy and arranged a fitting burial, the papacy now turns to democracy, to that wild heroine, as Father Ventura had called her, to those barbarians of the new era . . . It sees poverty, beloved by God, strength-giving, not niggardly when blood and sweat are at stake, as belonging to the future. That is why the papacy has gone over to the barbarians.' And Ozanam added: 'We too must turn to the barbarians and follow Pius IX'. This was a complete misreading of the actual Roman situation.

In any evaluation of the effects of the papacy on the modern world a distinction must therefore be drawn between events in Rome and the illusions to which these gave rise abroad. Not infrequently the illusions proved more important for the popes than did the facts. Outside Rome little was known, at least among Catholics, of the true conditions in the Papal States and of the excessive antagonism to all modern ideas which characterised the outlook of Gregory XVI and Pius IX as well as that of Lambruschini and Antonelli. These illusions about Rome were strengthened by two factors. There was the liberal-protestant campaign of defamation against Rome which produced so much nonsense that the real core of its accusations was no longer recognisable; and there was the obvious injustice done to Rome by Piedmont which concealed the true character of the Roman attitude. This injustice in fact gave to the reactionary political opinions of Pius IX and Antonelli the appearance of justified defensive measures. This became apparent in regard to the concept 'a free church in a free state' which Montalembert described as his political ideal. He regarded it as unworthy of the church to make use of force in her own defence. Indeed, like Lamennais, he believed that the church would succeed more easily within a liberal state than in any other. In his address at the Malines Catholic Congress of 1863, he described the task of the church as the reconciliation of liberalism and democracy, the protection of the individual, of associations and their liberties from the egalitarian tendencies of democracy. He saw the church as the fount of all liberties. But the only response to his appeal came from Antonelli who accused him of working for the same aim as Cavour who also demanded 'a free church in a free state'. After the Papal States had ceased to exist, Cavour too was prepared to grant to the church all the liberties which it was in the power of a free state to bestow. Rome, however, saw only the planned seizure of the Papal States disguised by liberal protestations and failed to recognise the underlying programme; anyone who used the slogan 'a free church in a free state' was suspected of sympathising with Cavour.

The liberal failure to influence the papacy

The liberal Catholic illusions about Rome were finally dispelled by the Syllabus (1864) and by the dogma of papal infallibility (1870). Suddenly the liberal Catholics saw themselves confronted by a Roman church which condemned all their political achievements as works of the devil and violently anathematised the liberal movement irrespective of its attitude towards the church, whether favourable or unfavourable. All their efforts to extend the rights of the church beyond those determined by concordats through the greater participation of Catholics in politics had been in vain. Not surprisingly, conservative and liberal Catholics in France and Germany were utterly divided over the interpretation of the Syllabus.

The conflict between liberal Catholics who regarded themselves as ultramontanes and the true papist ultramontanes was symbolised in France by Montalembert's *Correspondant* and Veuillot's *L'Univers*. In 1869 Veuillot called for the dogma of papal infallibility to be declared in its extreme form, while Dupanloup, Lacordaire and Montalembert rejected it outright. Doubting the political wisdom of the curia, they feared a spiritual dictatorship would arise in the Catholic church and this was precisely what Veuillot demanded. The discussion following the Syllabus and the First Vatican Council thus destroyed the unity of French ultramontane Catholicism and weakened its political force.

A similar conflict, though on a somewhat more theological level, took place in Germany where the extreme interpretation of the Syllabus was upheld by a Jesuit, Clemens Schrader, supported by Johann Baptist Heinrich, a prelate from Mainz, while the opposition was represented by Ketteler, who shared Dupanloup's objections to the dogma of infallibility. In Germany government and liberal public opinion responded to Pius IX with the *Kulturkampf* (cultural struggle). This term originally meant the conflict between government and church, but later came to mean the persecution of the church by the state.

Catholic participation in politics

That these conflicts occurred only in France, Germany and Italy is due to the fact that it was only in these three countries that serious attempts were made to decide political issues on the basis of Catholicism. In France Veuillot's attempts to form an alliance with Napoleon III resulted in the *Parti Catholique*. Finally between 1871 and 1879, an alliance against the Socialist revolution between conservative Catholics and liberal Catholics was formed in McMahon's *L'Ordre moral*. Frightened by the *Communards* of 1871, the French middle classes were even prepared to grant Catholic demands, such as a reform of the university and the edcucational system. Catholicism seemed to them to be the only effective defence against the proletarian revolution, a notion which Montalembert did much to sustain. By opposing such an alliance because it was condemned in the Syllabus, the ultramontanists indirectly promoted the victory of the French anti-Catholic establishment which deliberately made no distinction between the conservative-ultramontane supporters of *L'Univers* and liberal Catholics. It pointed to the attitude of the popes in Italy and the ultramontane interpretation of the Syllabus and accused Catholicism as such of wanting to undo the achievements of the French Revolution and to go back to monarchial absolutism. That sufficed to make *l'état laique* widely popular among French people. The German attempt to separate Catholics from Rome through the *Kulturkampf* failed in the last resort because Bismarck was compelled to recognise that his struggle against Catholicism and its political influence merely paved the way to revolution and threatened to undermine the social order on which his Empire was founded. The compromise finally reached under Leo XIII served to strengthen the political movement of German Catholics. Because it had proved its usefulness to Rome during the *Kulturkampf,* the Centre Party was accepted by her. In Italy the self-emasculation of political Catholicism led to the papal ban on Catholics taking part in elections; it promoted the dominance of anti-clerical liberalism and brought about a series of laws hostile to the church. This would certainly have been avoided if Catholics, particularly the liberal Catholics, could have had their share in forming political decisions. The attitude of the minority of bishops who voted against infallibility in the Vatican Council was certainly influenced by these political factors.

Fear of the socialist revolution caused liberal Catholics in France to join the liberals and to support the constitutional monarchy,

Pius ix proclaiming the dogma of the Immaculate Conception on 8 December 1854. This gave a new impetus to marian devotions, but alienated the Catholic church further from Protestant and Orthodox Christianity. Before proclaiming the dogma, Pius took the unusual step of calling the bishops of the world to give their opinion.

but they still could not go so far as to support a democracy based on universal suffrage. In Germany Ketteler and the Centre Party went one step further in accepting Lassalles' demand for universal suffrage, and success justified their policy. The Party benefited from the new electoral law introduced by Bismarck in the *Reichstag*. Nearly sixty members formed the parliamentary party in the first Diet, and by 1912 it had become the most powerful group in the *Reichstag,* partly on account of its support from the working class. The absence of such support in France contributed to the failure of French Catholics to exert any significant influence on parliamentary democracy. In their social policy too German and Belgian Catholics were far ahead of Rome. At a time when Pius ix still persisted in treating social problems as a matter mainly for Christian charity, requiring no further discussion after the condemnation of socialism by the Syllabus and the Vatican Council, Ketteler was already being hailed as a 'social bishop'.

Rome's splendid isolation

In these circumstances it was especially unfortunate that the French, Belgian and German Catholics failed to make their influence felt in Rome, for they could have shown the curia and the papacy what the emergent modern society really meant and thus helped to determine papal policy. But Rome remained its own standard of all things in an aura of grandiose sovereignty. The resulting misunderstandings created the oddly ambivalent impression that Rome was remote from the realities of time and place and yet, as it seemed to ultramontane Catholics, that she was at the same time the very bastion of truth. This ambivalence was reflected in the papal statements issued by the curia, the ambiguous language of which gave them a tone of superiority, although in fact the ambiguity arose from the curia's inadequate and over-theorised assessments of a situation.

Catholics thus totally failed to impress the nature of their problems upon the papacy in its Roman fastness and were therefore unable to influence the Roman government. Pius IX on the other hand was the first pope to strengthen his own position by making use of the high regard in which he was held among Catholics. His flight to Gaeta had aroused the world's sympathy and this left its mark on his outlook. It led to his support, fluctuating though it was, for the ultramontane parties. After 1850, he encouraged them repeatedly but did not clarify their status in the relations between state and church. He never recognised their political importance, and regarded them merely as a personal following which it was useful to rely on although he was highly suspicious of their policies and their role in international politics. This was the setting in which the proclamation of the dogma of the Immaculate Conception and the granting of papal protection for the grotto of the apparitions at Lourdes were widely welcomed. With Pius IX also began the practice of celebrating papal feastdays of a personal character (such as the golden jubilee of his priesthood in 1869) which were intended to demonstrate impressively the links between Catholics and the Holy Father. These links and the 'Peter's Pence', re-established in 1860, also formed the basis of the popes' financial independence after the end of the Papal States. Support came also from various Catholic voluntary associations which were originally formed to provide aid when the Papal States were under military threat, and to help the Holy Father in his needs.

The history of the papacy from 1831 to 1878 is a story both significant and depressing. Except for the short interlude from 1846 to 1848, the papacy grew ever more confident in its antagonism to the age. This reactionary attitude became an inherent part of the church and ultimately prevented it from exerting any kind of positive and formative influence.

The reign of Pius IX certainly has its impressive aspects. But his many widespread condemnations affected such varied issues as liberalism, pantheism, naturalism, absolute rationalism, indifferentism, communism, secret societies, bible societies, freedom of worship, free speech and many more besides. Ultimately Pius made no contribution to the social problems of human society nor to any of the great issues of his age.

Part 3

The exodus from the Catholic ghetto

Pope Leo XIII, here portrayed by Sir William Nicholson,
understood the modern world better than did his predecessors
and played an important part in leading the Catholic church
out of her self-imposed isolation. He also attempted
to reconcile French Catholics with the French Republic,
a policy which was slow in bearing fruit.

The news that the cardinal-chamberlain Gioacchino Pecci had been elected Pope Leo XIII on 20 February 1878 caused hardly a stir in world public opinion. But when, forty-four years and three pontificates later, Benedict XV died on 22 January 1922, this was a major world event. A widely-scorned institution in 1878, the papacy had during these decades regained its recognition and prestige. This was primarily the achievement of Pecci who, as Leo XIII, has an important place in the history of the church. Nevertheless, there are various reasons why he should be considered in this context together with Pius X (1903-14) and Benedict XV (1914-22). For it was only in their total achievement that these three popes managed to lead the papacy and the Catholic church back into its own century and to assure her influence on the world of the twentieth century. In this perspective Leo XIII and Benedict XV can be described as political popes who not only increased the prestige of the papacy but also made important decisions concerning the relationship of state and church. Pius X was politically incompetent and, in the modernist controversy, allowed himself to be persuaded by his advisers to show an intolerance that is hardly paralleled in the history of the papacy. Yet he became a great religious reformer who provided the spiritual support for Catholic renewal.

Where Pius IX had rejected the age uncompromisingly, Leo XIII tried to solve the problems of his time in a positive way. He failed in two major political questions and his disappointment over them explains the reactionary features which marked the end of his largely progressive pontificate. His hopes of bringing about even a partial restoration of the Papal States came to nothing nor was he able to prevent the ultimate clash between the Third French Republic and the Catholic church. His expectations were also disappointed on the religious question of a reunion with the Anglican and the Eastern Churches. That is why the members of the conclave of 1903, particularly Pius X, his unpolitically-minded successor, believed

that Leo's flexible diplomacy had made too many concessions to the age without getting anything in return. The new spirit of free enquiry which was beginning to stir everywhere in the church, not least in theological studies, caused concern among the Roman cardinals. What had remained hidden under Leo came into the open under Pius x. He was chiefly a pastor and had no experience of diplomacy or of the curial machinery, yet with refreshing vigour he tackled important issues such as the new codification of canon law, the reorganisation of the curia and the training of priests. In the second half of his pontificate, however, he became the pawn of the curia. It was they who instigated his highly questionable measures against the modernists and obtained his backing for further Roman centralisation, that is, for complete clerical control over the laity. Under Pius x Rome developed into a spiritual dictatorship, belatedly justifying the fears of Montalembert and others concerning the dogma of papal infallibility. Benedict xv, who was familiar with the workings of the curia, was easily able to check its extravagance. Through exemplary acts of charity during the First World War he raised the prestige of the papacy to a level which it could have reached in 1814 had it so wished. Benedict's successor, Pius xi, found himself confronted, as Pius vii had been in 1814, by the possibility of making a fresh start.

The three pontificates were also united by various common difficulties. In the first place there was the Italian problem. Leo xiii still believed that he might be able by diplomatic means to bring about the restoration of the Papal States. The solution seemed nearer under Pius x and Benedict xv, but their relations with Italy were also marked by their 'Babylonian captivity' with all the consequent disadvantages for state and church. In matters of theology the years between 1878 and 1922 brought final victory for neo-scholasticism and Thomism. This was the period when all powers finally became centralised in the curia. The dominant position of its administrative apparatus was assured by its continuity. Two quotations may illustrate how the relationship between flock and shepherds was envisaged. An Instruction to the Italian Christian Democrats issued by the Congregation for Extraordinary Ecclesiastical Affairs on 27 January 1902 stated:

In the pursuit of its programme Christian Democracy is bound to act in accordance with the authority of the church, in complete submission and obedience to the bishops and their representatives. In all matters concerning the religious interests and actions of the church in society, Catholic journalists and writers are expected to submit their reason and will to bishops and pope.

An unsigned article, entitled *Punti fermi*, in the *Osservatore Romano* of May 1959 declared: 'His [the Catholic's] private and public conduct, in every area of his activities, must be ruled by the laws, orientation and instruction of the hierarchy'.

Ever since the proclamation of the dogma of papal infallibility an aura of intellectual dictatorship has hovered menacingly over the Chair of Peter. Untrammelled absolutism was the inevitable product of the curia's administration of the Papal States. With the widening scope of its tasks this dictatorship increased. Today the pope is no longer able to supervise the affairs of his supreme office himself. He depends on advisers. As in other totalitarian systems, this dependence increases in proportion to the growth of the machinery's anonymity, for it is never the adviser but always the ruler who appears to the outside world. Before the proclamation of infallibility, the pope was the spiritual head of the church and the ruler of a small state; after 1870 he was a universal spiritual ruler expected to exert his authority on world-wide problems. This change is most evident under Leo XIII, who addressed the world with declarations and statements of views as no other pope had done before him. But at the same time the papacy's dependence on three factors: its spiritual authority, its position in the world at large and its involvement in Italian politics continued to pose problems.

7 The Babylonian captivity

Leo and the Italian question

Italian politics occupy a key position in the pontificate of Leo XIII. The principal aim of his diplomatic activity was to get the papal splinter state restored. In his endeavour to reach a settlement with Italy, however, Leo encountered the opposition of a powerful group in the college of cardinals prepared to support reconciliation only if the Papal States were reconstituted.

Papal relations with the Italian government were ruled by Leo's stubborn adherence to *Non expedit,* that is, his ban imposed on Italian Catholics taking part in elections. The great Catholic successes in the local elections, in which the Pope permitted Catholics to vote, make it seem probable that, if he had withdrawn this ban, Leo's efforts to reach a settlement would have succeeded. He was first urged to do this in 1884-5 by Gursi, a former Italian Jesuit, who wanted a Catholic party founded, if necessary even against the pope's ban. He was urged again in 1886 by the Roman Electoral Union, which submitted a long memorandum arguing the necessity of founding a conservative opposition party to fight the government's anti-clerical legislation. Bishop Scalabrini of Piacenza, for instance, held that only a Catholic party could, in the long run, achieve tolerable conditions for the Catholic church in Italy since the restoration of the Papal States was unthinkable. In March 1889 bishop Bonomelli of Cremona put forward the same opinion in the review *Rassegna Nazionale;* his article was placed on the Index and he was forced to modify his views. Leo XIII persisted in his *Non expedit.*

According to the pope, the Roman question was a matter of foreign policy and did not concern the participation of Catholics in politics. This participation was in any case strongly rejected by the curial cardinals who feared that they might become dependent on Catholic parliamentarians. Leo XIII saw the fall of the Papal States as the result of a masonic conspiracy rather than of his pre-

German cartoon of Leo XIII acting as arbitrator in the dispute
between Germany and Spain over the Caroline islands.
Bismarck flattered Leo's vanity by offering him this role.
In the caption, the pope is said to have pronounced a true
judgment of Solomon on the partition of the unfortunate victim
and both sides exclaim contentedly: 'Go on, keep cutting!'

Papſt Leo XIII. als Schiedsrichter in der Karolinenfrage
zwiſchen Deutſchland und Spanien fällt ein wahrhaft Salomoniſches
Urtheil über die Theilung des Schmerzenskindes, ſo daß beide
Parteien befriedigt ausrufen: Schneiden Sie zu!

decessor's mistaken policies. His views on the Roman question were
stated in his first encyclical on 21 April 1878, in the simultaneous
Instruction to cardinal Vanvitelli and again in the Instruction of 15
June 1887, addressed to the newly-appointed cardinal secretary of
state, Mariano Rampolla. These statements show that Leo was the
victim of his historical perspective. He based the justification for the
existence of the Papal States on their long history. His own proposal
was that he should surrender most of the old Papal States, retaining
only an area on the right bank of the Tiber extending to the sea, and
should join the Italian kingdom as a confederal prince. However, in a letter to cardinal Rampolla he demanded the restitution
of Rome and full sovereignty over the city. This at once caused the
Italian government to break off negotiations and to pass further
legislation directed against the church.

Leo XIII greeting William II, Emperor of Germany, in 1888. The tactlessness of the German group accompanying the emperor led to a deterioration of relations between the two sides. It also inspired Frederic Rolfe (Baron Corvo) to lampoon the audience in his novel *Hadrian VII*.

After these disappointments Leo tried to reach his goal by diplomatic means. Initially he sought the support of Germany and her ally, Austria-Hungary, the largest powers on the continent. Bismarck's interest in reconciling German Catholics with the Imperial government had increased with his painful experiences in the *Kulturkampf*, and he knew how to play upon the vanity of Leo XIII and on that of Monsignor Galimberti who for a time acted as their go-between. Anxious for a *Kulturkampf* settlement, Bismarck skilfully encouraged hopes that he would support at least a partial restitution of the Papal States and managed to obtain some concessions from the pope. But 'the great Chancellor', as Leo hailed him, was not really prepared to support the pope's demands on the Roman question. He remained loyal to the Triple Alliance of Germany, Austria-Hungary and Italy. He would promise his intervention in favour of the restitution of the Papal States only if Italy were to become a republic.

Leo XIII regarded German and Austrian friendship with Italy as the real reason for Bismarck's faint-hearted support of the papal aims. He therefore suggested to the German Chancellor and to William II, who paid a brief visit to the Vatican in 1888, that they should exchange the Italian alliance for a reconciliation with France, for which he proposed his good offices. When this proved unsuccessful, in 1896 he began to direct papal policy towards relations with France. Cardinal Rampolla has often been held responsible for this diplomatic realignment but Leo's own feelings for France were not without influence. The immediate effect was a further deterioration of Leo's relations with Italy, as France and Italy, never the best of friends, were at that time on particularly strained terms with one another.

The solemn inauguration in 1895 of the Garibaldi monument in Rome within sight of St Peter's. This was one of the many incidents in the war of provocation between the Italian State and the papacy.

Italy and Rome at loggerheads

It was not only due to reasons of foreign affairs that a war of attrition, for which both sides showed a particular aptitude, developed between the pope and the Italian government. Various resentments had accumulated since the beginning of the Italian movement for independence. Commemorative events and jubilees served each side as useful weapons to irritate the other. Papal jubilees had become occasions for demonstrations, suitably stage-managed by Leo, of Catholic loyalty to the Holy See. The Italian opposition, Freemasons and liberals, quickly retaliated. The hundredth anniversary of Voltaire's death was celebrated in 1878 with unusual ostentation. In 1882 Italians commemorated the Sicilian Vespers, Garibaldi and Arnold of Brescia; in 1889 they unveiled a monument to Giordano Bruno who had been burned as a heretic; on 20 September 1895 they celebrated the twenty-fifth anniversary of the Italian liberation of Rome. These events were deliberately intended to show up the pope as the obscurantist figure of the age. The 'celebrations' did not always pass without incident. During the unveiling ceremony of the statue to Giordano Bruno, the diplomatic corps accredited to the Holy See had to stand by to protect the pope from the excited mob. Ugly scenes occurred when, according to the pope's last wish, the body of Pius IX was taken to the cathedral of San Lorenzo on the night of 12 July 1881. Fanatical crowds abused the procession on its journey and even attempted to throw the pope's coffin into the Tiber. In 1891 a train bringing French workmen and their leader, Léon Harmel, on pilgrimage to Rome was ambushed. It was understandable that Leo XIII frequently thought he would have to leave the Eternal City. He applied to various governments to grant him exile after the scandal over the body of Pius IX, and again in subsequent years. The Viennese court professed its willingness in principle but told the pope through its ambassador that he

should take this grave step only in case of extreme emergency. It was a bitter disappointment to Leo XIII that Spain, Austria and Germany were not prepared to risk their friendship with Italy for his sake. Only France offered an asylum, which for various reasons he was unable to accept.

Leo countered the demonstrations of liberal Italy with a series of ecclesiastical festivities. There was the golden jubilee of his priesthood in 1888, and the thirteen hundredth anniversary in 1890 of the coronation of Pope Gregory the Great, one of the founders of the Papal States. In 1894, on the sixth hundredth anniversary of the Shrine of Loreto, a papal palace was erected there, in which the pope was hailed as rightful ruler. Finally, there was the Holy Year of 1900. These celebrations, not to mention minor events, throughout his pontificate, served to demonstrate to the Italian state the

Léon Harmel (1829–1915), called
'Le bon père', was a French industrialist
who established a model factory at
Val des Bois and promoted the pilgrimages
of French workers to Rome to pay homage
to the 'prisoner in the Vatican'.

international prestige which its 'prisoner in the Vatican' enjoyed. Seated on the *sedia gestatoria,* invested with all the emblems of a sovereign, Leo was acclaimed by crowds of pilgrims with the old cry *'Evviva il Papa Re'.* He missed no opportunity of drawing the attention of the pilgrims to his position and to the oppression of the Italian government. These ploys were sure to embarrass the government, particularly in its political plight at the turn of the century.

A gradual return to reality

Leo, whose only acquaintance with modern society dated back to his short stay in Brussels, failed to recognise that by prohibiting Italian Catholics from taking part in elections, he was encouraging the very forces hostile to Catholicism in Italy. With his conservative preconceptions, he never saw Italian politics as the product of his own mistakes but only as a conspiracy of Freemasons, and his isolation in the Vatican merely confirmed him in this attitude. Freemasonry seemed to him the greatest enemy of the church and he was as much preoccupied by this bogey as Pius x, his successor, was with his anxieties over a church threatened from within by modernist plots. In his concern over Freemasonry Leo allowed himself to be taken in by an impostor who, under the assumed name of Leo Taxil, published forged reports about an alleged masonic pope of satanism, and shamelessly exploited Catholic credulity. Although the hoax was discovered just before the Catholic anti-Freemasonry congress took place at Trent in 1896, Leo had become so involved in the matter that he could not help being compromised. The commission set up to investigate the affair tried to pass the blame on to the credulous attitude of German and French Catholic laymen but this merely caused ill feeling everywhere.

No progress had been made over the Italian question when Leo XIII died on 20 July 1903. His successor, Pius x, wanted to give the

blessing *urbi et orbi* ('to the city and the world') from the balcony
of St Peter's immediately after his election. But, as after Leo's
election, his cardinal-chamberlain prevented this gesture as not
being in accordance with the status of the 'prisoner in the Vatican'.
In his whole mental outlook Pius x was even less able than his
predecessor to understand the pluralist and democratic structure
of modern society, though as former patriarch of Venice he had at
least discovered the usefulness of Catholic participation in local
elections, which served him as a lesson for the future. Since he was
an Italian patriot and had never belonged to the curia, he was able
to tackle the Roman question without bias. In view of the socialist
gains, he relaxed the ban on voting, though retaining it in principle,
by allowing Catholics in special circumstances to take part in elections, for example when it was a matter of preventing an enemy of
the church from being elected. A group of twenty-four Catholic
representatives entered the Italian parliament in 1909, but they
lacked unity and were in any case confronted by a majority of 484
deputies. That the pope's attitude was not due to any real·under-
standing of democracy was shown by his downright rejection of all
attempts to found an Italian Catholic conservative party. In this
Pius x and his Spanish secretary of state, cardinal Merry del Val,
were not really motivated by political considerations. They were
more concerned with the curia's demand for the laity's strict submission to their bishops. As a Vatican statement of November 1904
put it: 'Non-participation in elections remains the general rule.
The prudence of the bishop may permit an exception in individual
cases so as to prevent a candidate hostile to the church from being
elected. Catholics, however, are not to stand as candidates.' When
Romolo Murri, a Catholic priest, advocated the founding of a non-
denominational conservative party, emphasising that pope and
bishops need not concern themselves with day-to-day politics, he
was disciplined and his writings were placed on the Index. The

clerical regime developing under Pius x extended strict control over various Catholic lay associations which at that time were being founded in Italy on German models. Church penalties were imposed on all Catholics who, in these associations, in the press or politics, advocated ideas of their own which diverged from those of the curia, and their writings were condemned. Catholic theological students were even forbidden to read newspapers. The 'Catholic Action' movement, founded by Leo XIII and promoted by Pius x, even at this early stage was the very opposite of a democratic institution in that it was not expected to act according to the will of its members but was intended to obtain political influence with the object of serving the interests and intrigues of the hierarchy.

On the whole, however, tension between the papacy and the Italian state was noticeably reduced under Pius x. Cardinal Capecelatro was able to state in 1909 that 'Italian Catholics fulfil their obligation as good Catholics, as citizens and Italian patriots in regard to their country as constituted at present'. However, democratic institutions were not understood and were still rejected, and this attitude continued to jeopardise Catholic relations with society. The breakthrough came with Benedict xv. In his first encyclical of 1 November 1914 he protested against the untenable situation in Rome and reaffirmed the papal claim for a restitution of the Papal States, but this was generally taken to mean that although the old claims had not been forgotten, no offensive against the Italian state was intended. Benedict xv had little opportunity to affect Italian political conditions during the First World War, especially as he was compelled to observe the strictest neutrality when Italy entered the war in 1915. The curia hoped that a peace settlement might be used to have the Papal States reconstituted, but these hopes were ruined by the agreement in London of 26 April 1915 in which a participation of the pope in the future peace settlement was made subject to the Italian government's consent. During the war the German press made some play with the suggestion that the central powers, if they were victorious, should restore the Papal States; this caused some embarrassment to the pope who was very anxious to remain neutral. The allies had already accused him of taking sides when he did not condemn the German invasion of Belgium and the atrocities committed there. Immediately after the end of the war a reconciliation with the Italian state seemed to be within reach. Through American mediation an agreement was reached on 1 June 1919 with the Italian Prime Minister Orlando that some territory should be given to the pope under the guarantee of the League of Nations; but it had yet to be settled whether this area should remain confined to the Vatican or extend to the Tiber. This agreement came to nothing because of the fall of the Orlando government and the subsequent press campaign against the papacy, but it was now clear that a restoration of the old Papal States, of which some members of the curia still dreamed, was impossible.

While his secretary of state cardinal Gasparri continued to uphold the ban on Catholic political groups, Benedict XV, on 20 January 1919, authorised the Sicilian priest Don Luigi Sturzo to found his *Partito Popolare*. Don Sturzo was told to avoid anything that might be interpreted as a Vatican intervention in party politics, and to draw up a programme on political, democratic and interdenominational lines. At the same time Benedict wisely withdrew the ban on Catholic participation in elections. The next elections were held in November 1919 and resulted in over a hundred seats and a key position in Italian politics for the *Partito Popolare*, but it was too late to save Italian democracy.

The papacy's acceptance that the Papal States were finally lost coincided with the return to normal conditions for Catholics in Italian politics. The senseless ban on Catholic political activity had been intended to undermine the stability of the Italian state. In actual fact it certainly damaged Italian democracy by preventing its acceptance among the people and by giving political responsibility to minorities hostile to Catholicism. The liberal cabinet of the new Italian kingdom governed with a parliamentary majority but not with the people's support. The people's participation in politics, the most important premise of all democracies, was not achieved. Under the simultaneous attack by communists and fascists which was to come, the representatives of the Italian middle classes had no political platform on which they could defend themselves. The pontificate of Benedict xv did no more than awaken Catholic hopes of playing a decisive political role, but time was too short for the shades of the past to be exorcised.

8 Modernism and integrism

Leo XIII was pledged, to an even greater extent than his predecessor Pius IX, to the philosophical teaching of neo-scholasticism and St Thomas Aquinas. In his encyclicals, which had a great influence on Catholicism, he repeatedly referred to St Thomas and described his teaching as the embodiment of the true Catholic faith. In the encyclical *Aeterni Patris* of 4 August 1879, he instructed all theological colleges and seminaries to make Thomism the basis of their studies. In Rome he founded in 1880 an academy for the interpretation and defence of Thomist thought. Leo was open-minded enough not to assign supremacy exclusively to Thomist and neo-scholastic ideas, but his support certainly encouraged the most obstinate elements in the curia, who regarded deviation from medieval Catholic thinking as the beginning of all errors. During Leo's reign the curia suppressed, or made suspect, any ideas that differed from their own and thus prepared for the triumph of neo-scholasticism under Pius X. Neo-scholasticism became hated for its supporters' intolerance towards other, more original theological schools; it regarded theology not as a science but as a kind of spiritual armoury.

Signs of this growing intolerance had already become apparent in Rome in the nineteen eighties. I have already referred to the condemnation of Rosmini by means of forged evidence. There were many similar cases in subsequent years. Leo's encyclical *Providentissimus Deus* (1893) and his decree setting up an ad hoc commission of three cardinals and theological advisers to act as a supreme tribunal in biblical disputes was still more unpopular. The growing atheist criticism of the bible may have justified defensive measures, but this commission was quite incapable of serving biblical scholarship. It had to decide on the suitability and truth of scholarly findings but was insufficiently equipped to do so. That this institution developed into a second Congregation of the Index under Pius X was perhaps inevitable. Although *Providentissimus Deus* made explicit allowance for criticism and progress in biblical research, the danger was further increased when a permanent biblical commission was established in 1903 with the task of guiding research and supervising Catholic scholars according to the principles of the church. It was from this quarter that the attacks in later years on Catholic theological scholarship mainly originated and inflicted lasting damage on Catholicism. When Baron von Hügel, the great English Catholic scholar, and friend of Alfred Loisy and George Tyrrel, visited Rome in 1896, he ascribed the hardening of the clerical outlook to the growing number of integrists in leading curial positions.

Modernism condemned

Great hopes for a reconciliation of the church with the modern world, particularly with the sciences, had been awakened by the brilliant encyclicals of Leo XIII and his support for scholarship; he was responsible for the opening of the Vatican archives. But all the time integrist theology was making progress in Rome, and after the turn of the century the integrists waited openly for the death of the aged pope. A foretaste of future events was the condemnation of Americanism in 1899. In a letter addressed to cardinal Gibbons of Baltimore, Leo condemned Americanism which he described as an adaptation of Catholic teaching to the *Zeitgeist*: the church was to be reconciled with the world by placing less emphasis on unpopular dogmas but without rejecting them completely. This was regarded by the pope as a heresy. He also condemned the limitation of the hierarchy's control over the laity which Americanism implied.

Leo's letter was based on misleading information provided by French reactionary circles. The condemnation was really aimed at similar ideas allegedly advocated by French liberal Catholics. Two conservative cardinals, Mazella and Satolli, had drafted the letter. The circumstances surrounding the condemnation of Americanism and later on, the modernist conflict form a pattern: in both cases an attitude of mind was elevated into an ideological system which as such did not exist. Making this point, cardinal Gibbons wrote in his reply: 'I do not believe that anywhere in this country can be found a single bishop, priest or even layman with some knowledge of his religion, who ever expressed such monstrosities'. The pope's letter would probably never have been written if it had been preceded, as had been the custom under Pius IX, by a thorough investigation and a hearing of those who were accused. However, as illustrated by the condemnations of Alfred Loisy in 1893 and of Hermann Schell in 1898, it was now no longer a matter of calling individual theologians to order but of completely excluding new ideas from the church. Loisy was removed from his teaching post at the Paris Institut Catholique because he denied the absolute inerrancy of the bible. He submitted and gave a reasoned account of his views, whereupon cardinal Rampolla conveyed to him the pope's satisfaction over his obedient attitude and suggested that he should apply his great talents to other fields of scholarship. This he refused to do.

Loisy had adopted the important text criticism of German Protestant biblical scholars in his first important work, *L'Histoire du canon de l'Ancien Testament*, Paris (1891). In *L'Évangile et l'Église*, Paris (1902), a Catholic's reply to Harnack's *Wesen des Christentums*, and in his commentary on the Gospel of St John, *Le quatrième Évangile*, Paris (1903), he made his greatest contribution to biblical scholarship. Today this is recognised by Catholics, but at that time it seemed to go far beyond the limits set by the biblical commission in Rome. Loisy's conflict with Rome arose from his attempt to analyse the content of the bible with the apparatus of modern scholarship. Hermann Schell, however, was condemned for his ideas on the reconciliation of science and religion which he developed in *Der Katholizismus als Prinzip des Fortschritts* ('Catholicism as the

Cardinal Gibbons (1834–1921), archbishop of
Baltimore. His intervention in 1887 on behalf of the
'Knights of Labor' saved the movement from
papal condemnation and helped to minimise
the harm done to American Catholicism
by Leo XIII's condemnation of Americanism.

Principle of Progress') (1897). He submitted to the Roman authorities, but worn out by constant suspicion and broken in spirit he died on 31 May 1906 at the age of fifty-six.

The tyranny of the curia

Pius X became pope in 1903. He was a man of entirely pastoral interests, totally helpless in the midst of the curial machinations. His attempt to reorganise the curia merely provoked its increased activity so as to divert his attention from the intended reforms. The phantom of a large-scale modernist conspiracy, originating in Germany and aiming at the destruction of the church, was conjured up before him by the curia. Under Pius X the curia for the first time held absolute sway. The Spanish cardinal secretary of state, Merry del Val, was no less baffled than his master by the Roman machinations.

The new trend first found expression in the decree *Lamentabili sanu exitu* of 3 July 1907, in which 65 statements on biblical exegesis and the history of dogma, taken mainly from the writings of Loisy, were condemned. At the same time a second Syllabus was published, this time against the errors of the modernists, condemning quite indiscriminately every new idea in theology or anything that might curtail the curia's influence in the spiritual and secular fields. The doctrine described as modernism in the decree and in the Syllabus had no real existence in this particular form. From a Catholic point of view, it was considered wrong to think of the dogmas of the church as changeable symbols of religious truth, or to over-emphasise the notion of progress as a decisive criteria in biblical criticism or the history of religion. But the concept of modernism was not intended to deal with these phenomena. Soon modernism was taken to mean any endeavour to adopt modern ideas or to deal with them in a positive way. The encyclical *Pascendi dominici gregis* of 8 September 1907 described modernism as the fount of all heresies. Among the authors of this encyclical was cardinal Billot, who many years later resigned his office because he was angered by the condemnation of the *Action Française,* the French right-wing movement.

This encyclical at first caused incredulous indignation. A group of Italian theologians proved in detail that none of the statements made in the encyclical could be ascribed to the modernists. But they were powerless, and indeed they confirmed Pius x even more strongly in his fears.

The Munich theologian, Joseph Schnitzer, said at the time:

Although the image of modernism as drawn by the encyclical *Pascendi* was described as accurate by those who were opposed to or unfamiliar with its ideas, those most intimately concerned, whose views were at stake, all agreed that it was a caricature in which they could not recognise themselves.

Georg Schwaigers, the German historian of the popes, wrote: 'The modernist views as portrayed by the encyclical *Pascendi* were not advocated in this way by any of the real or alleged modernists.'

Even before this decree was issued, on 7 March 1908, the feast of St Thomas Aquinas, Rome solemnly enacted Loisy's excommunication. His views were doubtless far in advance of his time, but he was a victim not only of Roman fears but also of the conservative-minded French hierarchy which, under the influence of nationalist feelings, criticised his close links with the German evangelical theological school. This was also made a criticism of Tyrrell, the second leader of the modernists, of whom it was said in Rome that he expressed the spirit of Döllinger. His fate was not entirely un-provoked by his own acid remarks, such as: 'The German origin of modernism is its chief crime in the eyes of Rome: it alone sufficed to condemn it without further ado'. Pius x actually referred re-peatedly to the pernicious influence of German learning on French theology. As late as 1950 Paul vi, then cardinal Montini, told Jean Guitton that Loisy had been under foreign influence as far as his errors were concerned. It was the more surprising that no Germans were excommunicated together with Loisy and Tyrrell.

The struggle against modernism was an attempt to exclude from Catholic theology methods of modern scholarship which had been keenly supported by Leo XIII, and to keep it within the recognisable limits of scholasticism. Condemnations were not infrequently influenced by the sarcastic criticism of the curial methods to which some of the modernists were prone.

In the case of Italians, political considerations sometimes played their part also. Romolo Murri, for example, scandalised the curia with his view that the cardinals should keep out of politics. After the *Lega Democratica Nazionale,* founded by him in 1904, was condemned by Pius X, in 1909 Murri himself was suspended and excommunicated because, though a priest, he had allowed himself to be elected to the Italian parliament. He was received back into the church by Pius XII in 1943.

In Italy and France professors were removed without mercy from their theological teaching posts. Everywhere the air was thick with suspicion and hardly anyone dared to speak his mind for fear he should be suspected of heresy. No theologian of renown was at that time safe from hostile attack unless he clearly sided with the neo-scholastic camp. Loyal Catholic scholars, secular priests, members of religious orders, and even bishops were wantonly accused of modernism. The meaning of the term was arbitrarily extended and was frequently made to include other sinister aberrations. Replying to a question in a learned review, the German church historian Albert Ehrhard wrote in 1908: 'The current Roman condemnations constitute a mortal threat to conscience and religious learning in the Catholic world. They are a sin against the Holy Spirit.' Ehrhard made many enemies with *Der Katholizismus und das 20 Jahrhundert*, ('Catholicism and the Twentieth Century') (1901), and was accused of being a reform Catholic and modernist, and deprived of his prelacy. Even so he remained loyal to the church.

Yet, in spite of the hunt for heretics, the success of the curia fell short of their expectations: only a few theologians who, by the criteria of the encyclical *Pascendi* could have been described as modernists, had been tracked down. On 1 September 1910, Pius x, therefore, issued a *Motu proprio* by which the so-called modernist oath was made obligatory for all priests. Theoretically this measure ought to have put an end to all further distrust: anyone taking the oath evidently removed himself from suspicion. Since nobody, however, felt that modernism as described in the encyclical could possibly refer to himself, there were only two possibilities: either that modernism was a chimera or that many Catholic priests were perjuring themselves. The latter possibility was readily assumed in the poisoned atmosphere in Rome, marked by constant fear of secret plots.

The papacy's secret service

This was the cue for the rise of integrism. The integrist Catholics had two aims. First, they were anxious that all questions of private and public life should have a religious answer. This implied that the cultural, social and political spheres were in the final resort subject to the authority of the church. Their second aim was to uncover those modernists who by taking the oath had managed to hide their true beliefs. Devoted to this detective task in Rome was Monsignor Umberto Benigni who, with the knowledge of Pope Pius x, set up a secret service, the *Sodalitium pianum,* which soon became one of the most notorious organisations of its kind on the continent. In letters written in his own hand, dated 5 July 1911 and 8 July 1913, Pius x confirmed the organisation, which had some thousand members, and placed it under the consistorial congregation. Each year Benigni received the pope's praise. Since, particularly in the last years of his pontificate, Pius x surrounded himself with known supporters of the integrist conspiracy, it can hardly be maintained that Benigni devised his schemes behind the pope's back. That he went beyond his assigned tasks, however, was revealed when some of his files fell into German hands in Belgium, in 1915. The files contained intimate personal information about leading Catholics including bishops, which was to be used when necessary. Benigni's press offices in Milan, Fribourg, Vienna, Berlin, Cologne, Brussels, Ghent and Paris produced a constant stream of personal attacks and calumnies which indirectly provided the enemies of the church with ample material for their attacks against Catholicism. As for the unfortunate victims, those who tried to defend themselves in Rome were not listened to. It was significant that when later the activities of the smear campaign organisers were curtailed, they themselves came into conflict with the church and, in contrast to the attitude of those whom they had suspected, flared up and accused her of weakening under attack from her enemies. This was true of Benigni's closest collaborators in Germany, Brunner, Schapen and Kaufmann, and the Abbé Vercesi, his chief agent for southern Europe, who later left the priesthood and the church. Benigni himself was dismissed by Benedict xv. Later he acted as an informer for Mussolini and supervised the Vatican mail on behalf of the Italian secret service.

The constant denunciations put an end to some of the most reputable learned journals of Catholic theology in Germany, Belgium, Italy, England and France. Catholics throughout the whole world were divided into two camps, one of which supported these machinations and regarded the church's hostility towards the age as one of her finest characteristics, and the other, which looked on helplessly while their fellow-Catholics supplied the enemies of church and papacy with their most powerful weapons.

In his blind zeal, Pius x not infrequently clashed also with governments. The anti-modernist oath provoked a storm of indignation in Germany. After a protest from cardinal Fischer of Cologne, professors of theology at German universities were dispensed from having to take the oath. The pope was also forced to retreat in an equally embarrassing manner, after his encyclical *Editae saepe* of 26 May 1910, commemorating the three-hundredth anniversary of Carlo Borromeo, in which he had described the reformers of the sixteenth century as 'proud rebels, enemies of the Cross of Christ, worldly-minded men whose God was their belly'. Strong protests came from Germany and Pius then authorised the *Osservatore Romano* to explain that he had not intended to offend non-Catholic Christians in Germany, or indeed their monarchs.

In all these utterances Pius x had the modernists in mind and he never tired of castigating them as the plague of the times. However, this picture of men tenaciously clinging to their errors from hatred of the church showed merely how little Pius x understood the nature of their views. For it was not 'despicable curiosity' or 'pride', as he wrote in *Pascendi,* which influenced most of them but their wish to defend the church and to demonstrate her true character to a world that regarded her with scorn. Ever since the eighteenth century endeavours of this kind have been the causes of heretical tendencies, and it is this very ambivalence which tragically marks Catholic intellectual life to this very day.

Robert Scherer wrote in the *Lexikon für Theologie und Kirche:*

The phenomenon of modernism can ultimately be understood only as a failure in the confrontation between theology and the modern sciences and philosophy. That this problem has still not been solved is demonstrated by the fact that even after the Second World War there have been dark hints of neo-modernism. One might add that this still unsolved problem reveals one of the main difficulties in the relations between the papacy and the modern world. Missed opportunities for renewal at the beginning of the nineteenth century created a deep traditional pattern which can be discarded only with

difficulty and which continues to poison the Catholic church's relationship
with the contemporary world that is surely no less God-given than all the
other ages that preceded it.

The positive achievements of Pius X

In this perspective the reign of Pius X appears one of the most
negative pontificates. But he became one of the founders of the
modern papacy through his great internal reforms of the church
as much as Leo XIII had been through his success in giving the
papacy its important position in international affairs.

Pius restored the Gregorian chant to the liturgy (1904) and he
re-organised and improved diocesan seminaries (1907). The reform
of canon law which he introduced was continued by the energetic
cardinal Gasparri, later secretary of state. The new code was published in 1917, when Benedict XV was pope, and came into force one
year later. It was in keeping with the times that in the new regulations
for the election of bishops, in which Rome now had a decisive say,
Roman centralisation was accentuated. Although the new *Codex
Iuris Canonici* lacked conceptual clarity, it was nevertheless a
tremendous achievement. The internal reform of the curia which
Pius X initiated did not reduce its dominating influence, but many
abuses were abolished by limiting the Roman congregations, by
the clearer demarcation of responsibilities, the separation of the
church's judiciary and administration and the introduction of a
special code for ecclesiastical officials.

In the pastoral field Pius X carried out a reform of the breviary,
(1911-15) and began a new era with his Communion Decree (1905)
which encouraged daily communion and thus enabled Catholic
laymen to participate in what had hitherto been the clergy's religious
privilege. Pius X was actually fulfilling demands which had originated
among Jansenist reformers in the eighteenth century for a more

active devotional life, and he was to prepare the ground for liturgical reform. He issued new regulations for papal elections which included instructions to the cardinals to observe the strictest secrecy, and he also reorganised the *Rota,* the most important of the church's tribunals of justice.

Pius X died on 20 August 1914. He was canonised in 1954 by his former secretary Pacelli, then Pius XII. Opinions about him are likely to be influenced by the importance one attaches to certain of his achievements. Politically he placed the church in great difficulties. The persecution of the modernists and the conspiracy of the integrists which he tolerated cast a dark shadow not only over his own reign but also over future pontificates. As an internal reformer of the church, however, he was responsible for new reforms that were a direct product of his own spirituality. They had a lasting effect up to the Second Vatican Council and much that has since become accepted in Catholic devotional life would probably not have developed in this way without them.

9 Church-state relations under Leo XIII, Pius X and Benedict XV

At the death of Pius IX the papacy's international relations were in a precarious state. In France, Catholics were divided into two opposing camps over the Syllabus and its interpretation. This had enabled the enemies of the church to take political decisions into their own hands. In Germany, where Catholicism was decried as a fifth column subservient to a foreign power, the *Kulturkampf* raged and seemed to devour all the progress which German Catholics had made in public life since 1848. In Austria the dogma of papal infallibility had led to the termination of the concordat of 1855. In all these countries the Catholic church faced a menacing situation.

Leo XIII was not in a position, even if he had wished, to disregard the dogma of papal infallibility, which had largely caused these hostile measures against the church. Relations with individual states could therefore be changed only by settlements which sacrificed the close links, modelled on *Mirari vos,* by which the papacy was tied to the monarchies and to the old social order. Leo wanted to improve relations with individual states by removing all obstacles that did not involve fundamental questions of doctrine.

Right-wing Catholicism in France

After the French experiments of *l'ordre moral,* the liberal Catholic forces willing to play their part in public affairs had been worn down in the struggle between the so-called Syllabus Catholics who rejected the republican regime and their anti-clerical opponents. But as the hopes for a restoration of the monarchy receded, those who regarded the gulf between parliamentary democracy and the Catholic church as unbridgeable gained the upper hand. Their attitude produced a certain disaffection which gave the semblance of justification to the government's anti-clerical legislation. The gulf widened as both camps accused each other of unpatriotic conduct. Catholics blamed the republicans for subverting the best traditions

Dreyfus with his lawyer Demenge. The Dreyfus case split France
in two, the Catholics siding with the army, the royalists and
the anti-semites against Dreyfus, while the republicans, socialists
and anti-clericals defended him. When Dreyfus was declared
innocent his defenders turned public opinion against
Catholicism and started a wave of persecutions against the church.

of France through their anti-church laws. Republicans charged the Catholics with wanting to upset the achievements of the French Revolution. In their dislike of the republic, the Syllabus Catholics implicated themselves in three damaging political adventures which showed their lack of political sense. There was the affair of General Boulanger whose abortive coup aiming at the establishment of a dictatorship had the support of all the anti-republican forces including Catholics. There was the Taxil affair by which many French prelates were made to believe in the alleged evil aims of Freemasonry, and finally there was the Dreyfus case, supported even by liberal Catholics, which was used by the Syllabus Catholics to organise a nation-wide anti-semitic campaign of the most infamous kind. French Catholic extremism found its final expression in Charles Maurras' royalist and ultra right-wing *Action Française*. In their rejection of parliamentary democracy the French Syllabus Catholics, who after all were merely expressing papal teaching, anticipated a development that was to drive many conservative Catholics into the arms of fascism or of fascist movements in other countries as well as France.

The Catholic social movement in France

Leo XIII was concerned about the effects of this French Catholic attitude since he realised that it sprang directly from the papal recommendations in *Mirari vos* and the Syllabus. In 1885 he therefore forbade the founding by Count Albert de Mun of a new conservative party that would have steered a radical anti-republican course. Instead Leo referred De Mun to the importance of the social question, the solution of which he regarded as paramount. The pope hoped that such a movement would appeal to sections of the French working classes and give French Catholicism the support that it needed. From the outset the social question dominated his efforts to

Albert Comte de Mun (1841–1913) was one of the early leaders of French Catholic social thought. He believed that the solution of the social question was to be found on the basis of a corporate system such as had existed in medieval times.

reconcile French Catholics with the republic, for both Leo XIII and De Mun were profoundly interested in social problems.

As prisoners of war in Germany after 1870-1 De Mun and his friend the Marquis de La Tour du Pin had become acquainted with Ketteler's ideas on the social question. The rising of the Commune which both helped to crush convinced them that the German bishop was right in believing that what had caused the masses to rise was the neglect by the upper classes of their social responsibilities. While Ketteler, however, always emphasised the self-reliance of the workers and for this reason supported Lassalle's demand for universal suffrage, De Mun and La Tour du Pin remained hostile to the parliamentary system. Accordingly they were not so much concerned with raising the workers' status as with persuading the ruling classes to spread the basic principle of all social order with which the Syllabus was concerned – De Mun and La Tour du Pin adhered to a narrow interpretation of this – and to remember the obligations of their high social position. De Mun's ideas found a wide response.

The Berlin Conference on the protection
of workers of 1890. This promoted
a new course in German social legislation
and anticipated Leo XIII's
declaration of Catholic social principles
in *Rerum novarum*.

Liberal Catholics, who had lost influence after the electoral defeat of 1877, came to realise through the bloody shock of the Communards, that Catholicism must show its concern for the masses.

True to their conservative attitude De Mun and La Tour du Pin were only able to envisage collaboration between employers and workers in their *cercles ouvriers* under the guidance of priests, with the workers serving as objects of charitable concern rather than as men capable of independent decisions. The breakthrough to working-class organisations exercising their own responsibilities was initiated by Léon Harmel, a French industralist, who not only created exemplary social institutions in his own textile factories, but also emphasised the men's independence, autonomy and equality with the employers. Harmel was against the concept of the corporate state that was advocated by De Mun. Behind it he rightly suspected anti-republican and anti-revolutionary trends. Harmel's efforts also found very much greater response abroad than did De Mun's *cercles* which in the main were confined to upper-class membership and found little support among the workers. Unlike De Mun, Harmel defended the workers' right to strike. His ideas served as a model for the *Volksverein,* the Catholic people's association founded in Germany in 1890 by Hitze and Windthorst, which had as its primary aim the improvement of the masses by means of comprehensive social reform and systematised institutions for their education and self-training. They were to become, as Hitze put it, 'economically, morally and mentally capable of co-operating in state and society as mature and responsible persons'.

Harmel became famous for the pilgrimages of workers to Rome which he organised and which helped both to cement close personal relations between the French workers and Leo XIII, and to promote interest in social questions in Rome. In a lenten pastoral letter of 1877, when still archbishop of Perugia, Leo had already indicated his special understanding of these questions. In his first encyclical

Quod apostolici muneris (1878) he warned against the dangers of socialism although at this time he had no constructive proposals of his own to offer. But in 1881 he willingly agreed with the idea of the church setting up a committee to examine social and political problems.

Leo's support of the working class

The preparatory studies of the committee had not yet been concluded when in 1890 Leo XIII decided for political reasons to draw up the encyclical *Rerum novarum*. One of his reasons was that a conference was about to be held under the auspices of the Emperor William II to consider the protection of workers' rights. A further reason was the Belgian-French conflict between the Catholic Universities of Louvain and Angers which Leo XIII was anxious to terminate to prevent further divisions in French Catholicism. Louvain supported Léon Harmel and De Mun in demanding legal protection for the workers; this was opposed by Charles Périn, a Louvain economist then teaching under the aegis of the bishop of Angers. The time seemed to have come for an authoritative papal statement. Catholics in Germany, France and Belgium were deeply concerned with the social question. In the United States cardinal Gibbons of Baltimore in 1887 caused a sensation when he defended the 'Knights of Labor' whom Rome suspected of fostering revolution and communism, but who had in fact done much for the protection of the labouring class. In Britain cardinal Manning's intervention in settling the London dock strike in 1889 was so successful that the dockers carried his picture with that of Karl Marx in one of their demonstrations.

What was new about *Rerum novarum* was that the church for the first time expressed basic principles intended to remove the prevailing prejudices against the workers. 'A small number of very rich men',

DE CONDITIONE OPIFICUM

LEO PP. XIII

VENERABILES FRATRES
SALUTEM ET APOSTOLICAM BENEDICTIONEM

RERUM novarum semel excitata cupidine, quae diu quidem commovet civitates, illud erat consecuturum ut commutationum studia a rationibus politicis in oeconomicarum cognatum genus aliquando defluerent. Revera nova industriae incrementa novisque euntes itineribus artes: mutatae dominorum et mercenariorum rationes mutuae: divitiarum in exiguo numero affluentia, in multitudine inopia: opificum cum de se confidentia maior, tum inter se necessitudo coniunctior, praeterea versi in deteriora mores, effecere, ut certamen erumperet.

In quo quanta rerum momenta vertantur, ex hoc apparet, quod animos habet acri expectatione suspensos: idemque ingenia exercet doctorum, concilia prudentum, conciones populi, legumlatorum iudicium, consilia principum, ut iam caussa nulla reperiatur tanta, quae teneat hominum studia vehementius.

Itaque, proposita Nobis Ecclesiae caussâ et salute communi, quod alias consuevimus, Venerabiles Fratres, datis ad vos litteris *de imperio politico, de libertate humana, de civitatum constitutione christiana*, aliisque non dissimili genere, quae ad refutandas opinionum fallacias opportuna videbantur, idem nunc faciendum *de conditione opificum* iisdem de caussis duximus. Genus hoc argumenti non semel iam per occasionem attigimus: in his tamen litteris totam data opera tractare quaestionem apostolici mune-

the encyclical stated, 'have been able to lay upon the teeming masses of the labouring poor a yoke little better than that of slavery itself'. Rejecting the socialist solution, the encyclical emphasised the worker's right to own property. Towards this aim state and church must co-operate. Almost the most important point of the encyclical was its support for the right of workers to form associations and to take independent action. The old view that the social question was simply a matter of human charity and alms-giving was thereby finally set aside. The right of workers to fight for a just wage with all legal means including strikes was recognised by an authority from which one would have least expected it. *Rerum novarum* was a great achievement. It marked the papacy's advance to the forefront of those who were trying to solve one of the most important problems facing the modern world. Leo XIII gave his full backing to the efforts of individual Catholic social reformers and protected them against malicious defamation from conservatives, for there was widespread opposition in the church as in society generally at that time to 'over-sentimentalising' social problems and to giving the workers special rights in their struggle against oppression.

Less well known than the social aspects of *Rerum novarum* is the role which Leo intended it to play in regard to the relationship between church and state. Leo's view of the state changed during his pontificate. At first, taking the medieval view of the relationship of church and state, he regarded the church as the legitimate and highest form of society. When the assassination of Tsar Alexander II in March 1881 shocked the world, he used the occasion for a general review of the sources of civil power, appealing to rulers to use the support offered by the church and to protect religion in the interests of the state itself. This was still the old line – Gregory XVI too had hailed the church as the best defence against revolution and subversion – but in *Immortale Dei* of 1 November 1885 Leo for the first time laid down the principle that the church was committed

Cardinal Manning's intervention in the dockers'
strike of 1889 is here seen by the *Punch*
cartoonist as benefiting the export drive.
The dockers expressed their gratitude
to the cardinal by carrying his picture
in procession beside that of Karl Marx.

"RAISING THE (TRADE) WIND."

Cardinal Manning. "THERE, THAT'S RIGHT! BOTH BE REASONABLE, AND WORK TOGETHER.
BLESS YOU, MY CHILDREN!"

to no particular form of government: 'provided that justice is safe-guarded, the nations are free to adopt that form of government which best accords either with their character or with their traditional customs and habits'.

The papacy's declaration of political neutrality

The encyclical *Libertas praestantissimum* of 20 June 1888 on human liberty once more set out the Catholic concept of state and society as distinct from the liberal concept. It declared that individual political liberty still required considerable restrictions although the so-called 'modern freedom' (of worship, of speech, of the press, of teaching and of conscience) had always been approved by the church in its positive aspect. The pope, nevertheless, emphasised that what was new about this freedom was that it was 'the sullied product of a revolutionary age and of man's unbounded urge for innovation'. In this respect Leo's traditional approach was wholly negative and he indicated that he had little trust in parliamentary democracy. A new trend can be detected in the encyclical *Sapientiae christianae* of 10 January 1890 on the duties of Christian citizens, in which he stated explicitly that obedience to the state ceased when the church was victimised by the state, or when citizens were re-quired to act contrary to the commandments of the church. In *Rerum novarum* he referred again to the church's neutrality over the choice of government: 'God has ordered the two powers, one guiding man's concern for heavenly things, the other for earthly things. Each in its own way is supreme, both have definite boundaries within which they must keep, boundaries which are determined by their nature and the task laid before them.' It was in this encyclical, rather than in *Graves de communi* which belongs to the end phase of his pontificate, that Leo came close to an acceptance of parliamentary democracy. 'Adhering to the teaching of the church and observing the commands of the gospel in their private lives, they [the Catholics] may and shall participate in public affairs,' except in certain special circumstances (by which Leo meant the Italian ones). Such participation was not inspired by a wish to 'register agreement with the evil of present-day public affairs but in order to guide these towards the real and true good of the state, animated by the intention of infusing the wisdom and strength of the Catholic religion like a life-giving force into the state'.

There is also evidence that Leo XIII came to accept, at least after 1885, the independence of Catholic political parties. Later he conceived of these parties as by their very nature pertaining to the public and not to the ecclesiastical sector. He considered that the German Centre Party and the Catholic parties in Belgium and Holland approached the ideal, since, although basically Catholic, they were not denominational parties in the real sense, and were free of ecclesiastical authority especially in political questions. But in regard to France he showed a different attitude, as we shall see, and rejected French Catholic parties.

The encyclical *Graves de communi* of 18 January 1901 was less concerned with democracy than with social conditions. It referred to the right of the individual to play a part in public affairs, but this was not meant in a political sense. This encyclical was evidently intended for the French situation where Leo was anxious to promote the reconciliation of Catholics with the Third Republic. Because of his consideration for the Syllabus Catholics, whose fanaticism was at the heart of all the difficulties, he could not bring himself to speak out for the Republic, but it was precisely this that was needed. On 12 November 1890, on the occasion of a dinner attended by French army and naval officers and civil officials in the archbishop's palace in Algiers, cardinal Lavigerie amazed his audience by toasting the Republic and called upon all French Catholics to support it loyally. He spoke with the pope's knowledge but he outraged the royalist

Catholics, who had not yet recovered from their disgrace in Boulanger's attempted coup. Leo XIII backed the cardinal with an encyclical dated 16 February 1892, entitled *Au milieu des solicitudes* and appealed to French Catholics both to accept the Republic and to fight with all legal and democratic means against its anti-Catholic legislation. The appeal was linked in France to a movement embracing clergy and laity alike, which gave itself the impressive name of *Democratie Chrétienne*. This organisation, in the spirit of *Rerum novarum,* published in the previous year, sought 'to leave aside the question of the form of government in favour of developing a legitimate policy of influencing legislation and strengthening the moral prestige of the church through increased political action'. The pope's encyclical was received by the Syllabus Catholics with extreme abuse; prayer meetings were even held for the enlightenment of the Holy Father whom they thought was deluded by the devil.

The failure in France

French conflicts were emphasised yet again in the policy known as *ralliement.* The aim of this policy was to end the association of Catholicism and monarchism, to rally Catholics to accept political democracy and to promote social reform. The movement also found support in Germany, Austria, Belgium, Britain and the United States. But papal officials were deeply frightened of what seemed to them an aspect of modernism, a reconciliation between the Catholic church and the modern world, with the church making more compromises than she should. The 'social pope', as Leo XIII was called – one remembers the term 'liberal pope' by which Pius IX had first been hailed – seemed about to fulfil the long repressed hopes of all progressive Catholics. There was no need for a new flight to Gaeta to escape this intellectual revolution. Leo XIII was certainly not a liberal merely to please others. He knew what he wanted and how far he could go. But he too was obliged to retreat in questions of social reform as in theological matters, where he paved the way for the intellectually reactionary pontificate of Pius x. His retreat was brought about partly by his lack of success in France.

The *ralliement* had failed to bring about the desired reconciliation, and this failure prevented the people, especially the workers, from supporting the *abbés démocrates,* as the priests who supported the Republic were ironically called. No one in France had sufficient faith in the *ralliement* for it to succeed. When Leo xiii barred bishop Fava of Grenoble from founding a Catholic party which would have favoured the Republic, many progressive Catholics were unable to understand that Leo wanted to keep priests out of politics and lost all confidence in the integrity of the pope's intentions. While the *abbés démocrates,* who in many respects were the forerunners of the worker-priests, threw themselves with enthusiasm into public affairs, some laymen did proceed to set up a Christian Democratic Party, but it was a failure because only a few of the leaders of the Catholic social movement supported it. Léon Harmel and De Mun had at that time declared themselves in favour of the Republic, but La Tour du Pin and many others continued to support the monarchy. The Christian Democratic Party had failed to get any substantial support from French Catholics and was defeated in the elections of 1898. This called a temporary halt to its activities. The *ralliement* finally came to grief over the Dreyfus affair. This divided France into two fanatical camps with the majority of French Catholics, largely for anti-semitic and nationalist reasons, ranged against Dreyfus. When Dreyfus was finally proved innocent his Catholic accusers found themselves and the church hopelessly compromised.

The Divinity Building of the new Catholic University at Washington, D.C., in 1889. After initial difficulties with Rome because of its alleged Americanism – bishop Vane, the first dean, had to resign in 1894 – the university became the intellectual centre of American Catholicism.

The separation of church and state in France

After this French Catholicism, tainted for a long time to come with the odium of the Dreyfus affair, lost all political influence. The church drifted into trouble which even Rampolla could probably not have prevented had he been elected pope. But he might have obtained a greater measure of freedom for the church in France, and thus avoided the losses suffered by the French church through the rigid policy of Pius x. The following minor incidents were used by the French government as an excuse for the long-planned legislation to separate church and state. A sharp protest from Pius x against the Rome visit of the French president was followed by other small disagreements, particularly over the nomination of two bishops, whom the government wished to appoint without first consulting the pope. This led to the breaking-off of diplomatic relations on 13 July 1904. The law of separation of the church and state was passed by the chamber on 3 July 1905 and ratified by the senate on 6 December. The French law was clearly intended as an act hostile to the church; it was preceded by the closure of Catholic congregations and by other restrictions. The concordat was abrogated, the church's political position destroyed. With the withdrawal of financial provisions for religious orders, the confiscation of endowments, the drawing up of church inventories and their transfer to public associations or the local government, the Catholic church in France was deprived of all her rights and reduced to the status of a private association. For monarchist Catholics all this merely served as a confirmation of what they had always expected from the Republic and they called for outright resistance; but democratic Catholics tried to make the best of a bad situation by taking part in the associations of laymen provided by the law to conserve the ownership of the church's property. Hesitating only briefly, Pius x backed the conservative Catholics and, contrary to the advice of the

MISS MARY GWENDOLEN CALDWELL.

French episcopate, condemned the law of separation on 10 August 1906. In consequence the church lost all her own possessions in addition to the money the state had provided.

Another setback for the cause of Christian democracy in France was the failure of *Le Sillon,* the movement founded in 1894 by Marc Sangnier with the aim of getting young people to live a Catholic life as individuals and as members of society. Sangnier had an ardent faith in democracy and hoped to overcome the barriers of class and religion by contact and discussion between Catholics and non-Catholics. He extended his activity to the social and political spheres and gathered around him men from all walks of life to fight the anti-Catholic legislation. He was commended for his work by Leo XIII but his organisation fell victim to the new integrist policy which the pope's death accelerated. The French church authorities thought that Sangnier was trying to remove Catholics, both laymen and priests, from the authority of the bishops. They could not tolerate this nor his dangerous belief that Christianity could imply democracy. The condemnation of *Le Sillon* in 1910 clearly favoured the anti-semitic, anti-democratic, and monarchist *Action Française* which had long enjoyed Pius' sympathies. When some of the books of Charles Maurras were put on the Index on 26 January 1914, Pius X decided, contrary to usual practice, not to promulgate this condemnation because he felt that despite his errors Maurras had helped the church in fighting modernism and *Le Sillon*.

The heresy hunts conducted by the integrists took on particularly unpleasant forms in France through their conservative and royalist Catholic support; they naturally added to the bad reputation of Catholics and seemed to justify the state's measures against them. Matters improved only after the outbreak of the First World War, although the government had long tried by a more liberal interpretation of the anti-church laws to take the sting out of the tense situation. The decade following 1914, however, was to prove that the church in France derived benefits as well as disadvantages from the separation of state and church, not the least being her greater independence from the state, which had fruitful effects in many fields. The policy of *ralliement* and its failure demonstrated clearly that Leo's insistence on the church's neutrality in regard to particular forms of government existed only in theory. In regard to the European monarchies Catholics were expected to show their loyalty as citizens, but in regard to the democracies, the church, inspired by ignorance or long-standing animosity, denied Catholics their basic right of political participation. The Italian situation was at the root of this, for the church could hardly approve of democracy in France and, at the same time, ban Catholic participation in elections in Italy. The liberal anti-Catholic regimes in Italy and France were merely reacting to Catholic antagonism to the times, providing a logical opposition to Syllabus policy. In that situation even the more liberal attitude of Leo XIII proved ineffective because in the last resort he was not convinced that the church could actually tolerate differing forms of government.

Overleaf European political boundaries
1908–11 and the percentage of Catholics
in the population of each country before 1914.

The church-state relation in other countries

This explains why the situation of permanent conflict which existed
in Italy, France and Spain and many other countries could be
avoided in other countries only when the church and state could
agree to disagree about the form of government. This is what happened in the United States, Britain, Belgium and Holland where the
Catholic church was not tied to the state and Catholics who were
anxious to protect the interests of the church had to play their part
in public affairs. This was the case also in the constitutional monarchies, such as Germany and Austria, where Catholic parties had
proved themselves in exceptional situations. The return to a reactionary attitude under Pius X, however, was bound to create new
difficulties even in these countries.

That is why the social teaching of Leo XIII, which was certainly
his main contribution towards a solution of modern problems, had
a far greater appeal in these countries than in France, Italy and
other countries with conditions of conflict. In Britain, where the
majority of Catholics belonged to the working class, the papal
teaching on the social problem helped to increase the prestige of
Catholicism. In the United States Catholics found a great leader in
cardinal Gibbons, who openly criticised the papal condemnation
of Americanism and lent his prestige to the support of *Rerum
novarum*. He played an influential role as adviser to President
Cleveland and President Theodore Roosevelt. It was due to him
that the Catholic University in Washington, which soon exercised
an important influence in American Catholic intellectual life, was
founded in 1887. Supported by the American hierarchy, cardinal
Gibbons succeeded in 1887 in securing a suspension of two condemnations of the 'Knights of Labor'. Ecclesiastical authority,
cardinal Gibbons wrote in a famous letter, ought 'to acknowledge
frankly what is true and just' in the cause of workers 'in order to

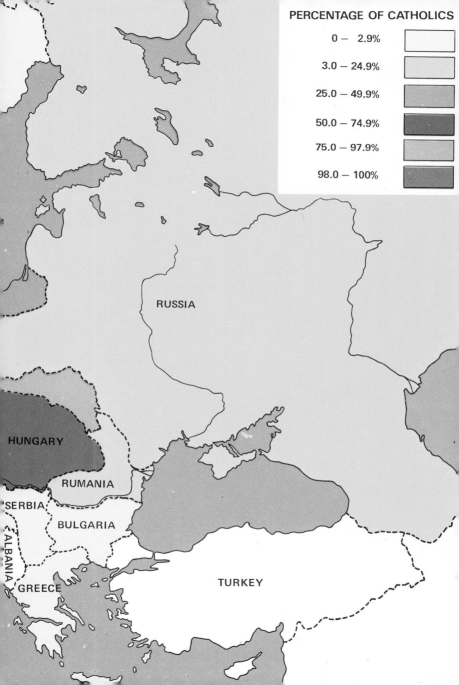

PERCENTAGE OF CATHOLICS

0 — 2.9%	
3.0 — 24.9%	
25.0 — 49.9%	
50.0 — 74.9%	
75.0 — 97.9%	
98.0 — 100%	

RUSSIA

HUNGARY

RUMANIA

SERBIA

BULGARIA

ALBANIA

GREECE

TURKEY

deter them from what is false and criminal, and thus to turn into a legitimate, peaceable and beneficent contest what might easily, by a course of repulsive severity, become for the masses of our people a dread volcanic force like that which society fears and the church deplores in Europe'.

The American Catholic social movement owed much to the ideas on industrial democracy in the form of worker participation in management and ownership which the Reverend John A. Ryan of the Catholic University of Washington propagated in *A Living Wage* (1906) and other later writings on the lines of *Rerum novarum*. Ryan believed that, although Catholics could not compromise with the materialistic philosophy of socialism, economic socialism was as valid and permissible a theory as any other. The church must show sympathy and understanding for the broad movement of economic democracy if this system was not to become more and more unchristian. But when in February 1919 the Bishops' Program of Social Reconstruction was issued, which called for radical social and political reforms, reactionary Catholic opposition to Ryan and his group hardened in the general American post-war fear of communist revolution. The National Catholic Welfare Conference was founded in 1922 to continue Catholic war and peace-time efforts to co-ordinate the working forces of the church for industrial reform, civic education and social service; it developed into a unifying force of American Catholicism.

Model Catholic organisations in Germany

In Germany the situation was different. A Catholic political party led by laymen and a powerful lay organisation, the *Volksverein,* gave Catholicism a powerful position. In 1886 the *Kulturkampf* was ended by a diplomatic settlement. Although this was not altogether acceptable either to the Centre Party or to Catholics generally,

Catholic associations soon began to flourish. A strong interest in social questions which German Catholicism had inherited from the time of Bishop Ketteler, found expression in self-governing workers' associations. The foundation of the *Volksverein* in 1890, and the encyclical *Rerum novarum*, which was enthusiastically received, accelerated these trends. German Catholicism became a model to the outside world through its excellent organisation. It was therefore relatively independent of the views of the state developed in Leo's encyclicals. These encyclicals were received with approval but it did not occur to anyone to question existing conditions.

When in 1901 *Graves de communi* interpreted Christian democracy in a non-political sense, German Catholics thought that in their *Volksverein* they possessed a ready-made example of Leo XIII's ideas. They considered themselves proudly as the most loyal and progressive sons of the church. This attitude changed only when, under Pius X, German Catholicism became a special target for integrist calumny and attack and some zealots felt they owed greater loyalty to Rome than to their Centre Party and the *Volksverein*.

There are various reasons for this development. In Germany the pontificate of Leo XIII was regarded as particularly advanced in spite of Rampolla's pro-French policy; it produced a very active Catholic cultural movement which affected all branches of public life. German Catholic scholarship flourished again: it was realised that the hitherto inadequate Catholic participation in the sciences and humanities was a result not only of the world's antagonism towards the Catholic church, but also of Catholic indifference to learning generally, and of a kind of inferiority complex. The Görres Society, founded by Georg von Hertling for the promotion of the sciences in 1876, and the Leo Society, founded in Austria in 1892, greatly increased their activities at the turn of the century. A new generation of Catholic intellectuals sought to apply a new understanding of Catholicism in different fields. In 1903 Carl Muth founded the review *Hochland,* which under his editorship until 1941 tried to end the cultural isolation of Catholics, as the *Correspondant* had done in France.

In Rome very different opinions were held. The books of Hermann Schell, who fought for a Catholic reconciliation with modern culture, had, with some manipulation, just been placed on the Index. But there were also Germans who distrusted the new spirit and who were ready to act as informers. They agreed with the Roman view that Germany was the hotbed of modernism, and that France had become infected with the German disease.

Rome also disapproved of the independence of episcopal control enjoyed by the German Catholic associations. This disapproval was shared by some of the German bishops, particularly by cardinal Georg von Kopp of Breslau who had played a prominent part in terminating the *Kulturkampf*. The conflict which finally divided German Catholics into two camps arose from the so-called trade union dispute.

Catholic workers' associations had been founded in Germany in the eighteen-eighties by Franz Hitze; by 1889 there were already 165. The idea of founding a unified trade union movement had to be dropped in 1902 because the alliance between German Social Democrats and trade unions had become so close that the non-socialist workers no longer felt their interests would be represented by it. Christian unions had previously been founded by the miners (1897) and the textile workers (1898). They tried to model themselves on the British trade unions. From the beginning the aim, unlike that of the Catholic workers' associations, was to create non-denominational Christian organisations. Unions with such mixed denominational membership were founded at that time in many different trades. At the turn of the century these flourishing Christian trade unions had almost complete Catholic support. Trouble arose, however, when the Christian organisations, which were supported by the *Volksverein*, joined in strike action. One of the leaders of the *Volksverein*,

Heinrich Brauns, later minister of social welfare in the Weimar Republic, defended the unions in the Catholic *Kölnische Volks-zeitung* against the objections put forward by moral theologians and other ecclesiastics. But Catholic integrists were scandalised, increasingly so after 1906, by the mixed-denominational character of these trade unions and by the fact that they were not controlled by the clergy.

This disagreement greatly damaged the Catholic cause in Germany. Pius X decided on 24 September 1912 that the German bishops should allow Catholic workers to belong to non-denominational unions if there were good reasons for doing so. The conflict was never finally settled and was swept aside by the First World War.

Similar developments took place in Austria where the Catholic *Volksbund,* which resembled the German *Volksverein,* was founded in 1909. The Austrian Christian social movement led by Lueger had partly militant nationalist and anti-semitic aims and was comparable in its political importance to the German Centre Party.

The death of Pius X and the outbreak of the First World War saved the papacy from great difficulties. It attained new heights of world prestige during the pontificate of Benedict XV, the diplomatist and disciple of Rampolla. Benedict failed in his great peace mission of 1917, with which Pacelli, then nuncio in Munich, was closely associated, largely because of the German refusal to evacuate Belgium. The pope was accused by both sides of having violated his neutrality in favour of the enemy. But its efforts to alleviate suffering and to help prisoners of war heightened respect for the Holy See. Benedict XV also added to his moral stature by his well-founded criticism of the Paris Treaties.

Leo's belief, considered suspect under Pius X, that the church must show favour to no particular government, was now fully vindicated. It enabled Catholics in defeated Germany and Austria to play their part as patriots in the reconstruction of their countries and in assuming political responsibilities. But there was still resistance. A conservative minority among German Catholics rejected the Weimer constitution because it began with the words: 'All power derives from the people'. Benedict XV helped to meet their objections. With the founding of a Catholic party in Italy which he encouraged, the Catholic church seemed set for reconciliation with parliamentary democracy. Unfortunately, as the following years were to show, the foundations which Leo XIII had built for this purpose were inadequate. But at least when Benedict XV died in 1922 there were the same hopeful possibilities for progress as there had been at the death of Pius VII a hundred years earlier. The situation was even more favourable after Benedict since he had skilfully prepared the way for a reconciliation with France and had done much to smooth the church's path in the newly-formed nations of eastern Europe. In France the ice was broken by the canonisation of Joan of Arc on 16 May 1920, which prefaced the resumption of diplomatic relations in 1921. In Czechoslovakia matters were helped by the removal of bishops unacceptable to the new government, such as Count Huyn, the archbishop of Prague. One of Benedict XV's most considerable achievements was his success in weathering the European upheavals of 1918-19 without major conflict for the church in any of the newly-formed states.

Part 4

Papal absolutism
1922-63

Achille Ratti, archbishop of Milan, became pope on 6 February 1922. It was not an easy office for him and it certainly had not become an easier one by 1963, when Giovanni Montini, also archbishop of Milan, followed him to the papal throne. The papacy's position in international affairs had been transformed in the interim. When Achille Ratti adopted the name of Pius XI, the papacy had already secured its place in the world. The Catholic church was still a most conservative power, widely respected, but with hardly any influence beyond her own members. It was doubtful whether Benedict's great diplomatic skill had really ushered in an era of papal open-mindedness towards world problems. When Montini was elected pope, the church was in the midst of revolutionary changes, greater than any she had experienced since the Council of Trent.

The short pontificate of Benedict XV had opened up new possibilities for the papacy, but he made hardly one single important decision nor did he determine a future course of events. He put a stop to the machinations of the integrists, but Benigni was still at the Vatican and his supporters were still occupying important positions in the curia. Benedict XV had declared his readiness to solve the Roman question but the negotiations had not gone beyond the early stages. Against the advice of his secretary of state, cardinal Gasparri, he had encouraged Don Sturzo to found his *Partito Popolare,* which was Catholic in aims but otherwise modelled on the non-denominational lines of the German Centre Party. Yet, when the pope died, the Italian party was unable to cope with the anti-democratic prejudices of Italian prelates and the clerical attempts at domination.

The church was estranged from the world of 1922 for three reasons. In the first place a number of new states had taken the place of Catholic Austria and initially showed hostility towards the papacy on account of its close links with Austria-Hungary. Secondly the papacy faced a liberal, pluralist western world such as it had consistently opposed since the time of the French Revolution. The defeat of the central powers and the disappearance of the German monarchies deprived Rome of partners in the traditional links of throne and altar. Their place was now taken by the French model which for various reasons Rome had always rejected. Thirdly, Rome was again confronted with a Protestant or rather Calvinist puritan world. The worldly, materialist character of its social ideals seemed to challenge the Catholic theory of social order in which success, wealth and social position counted for little. A connected phenomenon was that, generally speaking, Catholic populations lived under worse social conditions than those of other faiths. The belief that what really mattered was the life beyond and its rewards for all the wrongs which man suffers on earth was diametrically opposed to the outlook of the modern world, whether capitalist or socialist. This may or may not have been the end result of the voluntary retreat from the world practised by Catholics in the nineteenth century, but these three reasons together certainly explain why, from the papal point of view, the world had changed for the worse. In spite of the papacy's increased prestige, it could hardly identify itself unreservedly with the world as it emerged from the First World War.

Mindful of the lessons of the past fifty years, especially those of Leo's pontificate, Rome embarked upon a policy that oddly combined acceptance and rejection of the world. It ended in the unparalleled papal absolutism of Pius XI and Pius XII. This absolutism, reflected generally by Catholics in their views on their church, was based above all on Leo's political teaching, on the concordats and on 'Catholic Action', that is, the movement of laymen led by the hierarchy. (This movement must be clearly distinguished from the activity of the laity in the nineteenth and indeed in the twentieth centuries which tended to break away from hierarchical control and strive towards democratic forms.) These three cornerstones proved to be shaky ones when the church had to face the critical test of fascism. This in turn brought the papacy to a critical turning-point which was disguised at first by the dominating personalities of Pius XI and Pius XII, but which was finally confronted in the Second Vatican Council.

10 The teaching of Leo XIII on the state

Leo XIII enabled the Catholic church to adopt a positive attitude towards different political systems. But his encyclicals did not cover all the problems of modern society and all aspects of church-state relations. Important questions such as the control of government, the liberties granted by the state to its citizens, the question of whether or not there ought to be a 'Christian' state – all these were left open. Leo, in fact, was far from achieving the programme for Christian democracy which Lamennais had outlined, or indeed any programme which liberal Catholics would have expected as a matter of course from a political system of their choice. When Leo XIII finally adopted the term Christian democracy, he used it, in consideration of the French situation, in an unpolitical, social sense. The ideal of the Catholic citizen acting on his own political responsibility and playing his part in society was not for him. His teaching was powerless against a system which promised to respect the rights of the church, as Hitler promised in 1933. The truth was that Leo XIII had not really gone into the problems of modern society but merely insisted on special privileges for Catholics concerning their religious practice. How Catholics should respond to the demands of the anti-Christian totalitarian state was their affair. In theory they had the right to resist the demands of such a state, but they were not told how totalitarian oppression might be avoided. Considering the power of the totalitarian state, the right to resist it amounted virtually to martyrdom, as events in the twentieth century were to confirm. Leo had nothing to say in his doctrine on the state concerning the political responsibility of Catholics. This defect qualified the effects of an otherwise remarkable pontificate.

The pope's failure to recognise specific features of the modern world was certainly due in part to the low intellectual calibre of his advisers. The Thomist doctrine on the state had been based on the assumption of a Christian world order. In emphasising her own neutrality regarding different forms of government the church now proceeded on the quite unwarranted assumption that she could co-exist in a similarly neutral world order. Although there was continual reference to a world hostile to Christianity and to the dangers arising from it, nothing was done to prevent Catholicism in public life from being victimised by anti-Christian forces. And what these forces were really like, it was left to the twentieth century to reveal. Leo XIII believed he had sufficiently accounted for the modern world by pointing to nineteen centuries of church-state relations, by leading the church back to political neutrality, and expecting Catholics to make their own arrangements with particular forms of government, even with democracy. This defect was later widely felt. It explains why it was that in the nineteen twenties ideas about the corporate state came into their own again, as they had been developed in the 1880s by De Mun in France and by Karl von Vogelsang in Austria. These ideas were put forward by Pius XI in the encyclical *Quadragesimo anno* of 1931 but earlier Leo XIII rejected them as impracticable. The helplessness of the anti-parliamentary forces, among which Pius XI must be included, undoubtedly facilitated the rise of fascism.

After 1918 the Catholic parties in Austria and Germany discarded the traditional link of throne and altar and were able to play their part in the new political order. But it soon became clear that, while joining in political responsibility, they did not really accept the democratic system as such. Though political neutrality may imply positive assent in some systems, in a democracy it usually means the opposite. The European Catholic parties made this discovery only when events increasingly hostile to democracy revealed their inability to save it. For Leo XIII the church's recognition of a particular political regime presupposed three requirements: its permanence, its renunciation of all legislation against the church and its resolve to remain part of what was called the Christian family of nations. General criteria of this sort were of course unlikely to reveal the real aims of the German and Italian dictatorships. These dictatorships were in any case anxious to conceal their aims from their own people and from the world at large. The popes, therefore, in the early stages of fascism had already become unwitting abettors of regimes which in their essence were incomparably more unchristian and hostile to the church than liberalism, which Rome still regarded as the chief enemy, had ever been.

11 The concordats

After 1920, as after 1815, the curia placed its trust in a policy of concordats concluded with individual governments. These legal settlements were really an anachronism in modern government. The special status negotiated for Catholics was contrary to the equality of all citizens before the law. The rights of the Catholic church were placed above changing social conditions, so that governments lacked, in regard to their own Catholic citizens, the flexibility which is one of the chief assets of democracy. The concordats thus ignored democratic procedure by frequently making settlements without consulting the Catholic citizens concerned; sometimes they sanctioned terms that were unrealistic in regard to the social situation of a particular country and the interests of its Catholic population. That this was something against the nature of modern pluralist society became apparent during the Second Vatican Council. When religious freedom was debated, various speakers objected that a declaration in its favour would preclude Catholics in future from obtaining special status, and would put an end to the concordat system altogether. This was opposed by those who defended the right of Catholics to practise their religions as freely as other denominations in a pluralist society. They considered that mere legal privilege was meaningless in the modern context.

It was obviously desirable to draw up agreements with newly-formed countries. But although concordats had originally been special settlements, they became the normal pattern after 1922. And the curia's natural wish to reach agreements particularly favourable to itself often prevailed over consideration of social and political conditions in the countries concerned. In his *Ius concordatiarum pii* (1929) Ottaviani, later much maligned as an ultra-conservative cardinal, elevated the concordat policy into a political system. Altogether more than forty concordats and ecclesiastical treaties were signed under Pius XI and Pius XII. The curial diplomats built a network of treaties in which they themselves were finally trapped, since

Cardinal Gaspari, secretary of state
to Pius XI, and Mussolini signing
the Lateran treaty (11 February 1929)
which ended the conflict between the
Catholic church and the Italian State.

these treaties not only encouraged anti-Catholic feeling in many
countries but also established rights that could not always be secured,
thereby emphasising the powerlessness of the curia.

The problems of the Napoleonic concordat were thus repeated.
Hitler and Mussolini were of course more concerned with reaching
an agreement with the Vatican than with the actual contents of that
agreement. Rome was not blind to this factor and included it in
her calculations. As the old Roman proverb puts it, 'governments
pass away, documents stay'. The cardinal secretary of state Pacelli
told the British minister to the Holy See in 1933 that the church had
no choice but to sign the concordat with Hitler's Germany, since
no democratic German government had ever offered her such
favourable terms.

Once these treaties had been ratified, the church, practically bereft
of her defences, was exposed to the full attack of the dictators.
Hitler never intended to observe the treaties, Mussolini always tied
them to particular conditions. They finally proved to be not only

Der Stürmer

Neue Fortsetzung
Im Judenparadies

...sches Wochenblatt zum Kampfe um die Wahrheit

HERAUSGEBER · JULIUS STREICHER

46   Nürnberg, im November 1936   1936

Seine Diener
tragen goldbestickte Hüte und Brüsseler Spitzen —
sie werden daran sterben, daß sie Juda nicht erkennen

Im schwarzen Schatten
Niemals auf zur Sonne blicken.
Immer nur die Rücken bücken,
daß auf dieser schönen Welt
Keinem es zu gut gefällt

Paulus
Nebbich, es hat sich für die Juden rentiert, daß aus
dem Saulus ein Paulus wurde

Aufklärung im Beichtstuhl
O mei, Hochwürden die Sünden, nach denen Sie
mich fragen, kenn ich noch nicht

Anti-religious cartoons from the Nazi
weekly *Der Stürmer* (November 1936)
published by Julius Streicher.
A low-quality onslaught on Judaism
and on Christianity in general.

185

hopelessly inadequate but a burden for the church. But Pius XI
and Pius XII considered the rights ceded to them by the concordats
as more important than Catholic political participation; they sacrificed the Catholic parties, deliberately in the case of the *Partito
Popolare,* perhaps involuntarily in the case of the German Centre
Party. For these agreements the papacy paid heavily in loss of
prestige. It survived persecutions by these regimes – the first modern
anti-Christian states besides the Soviet Union – only because they resorted to war and over-taxed their strength. Pius XI and Pius XII
seemed to believe that they were still living in the nineteenth century,
that is, that they were faced with governments not hostile but merely
indifferent to religion. They had to learn that the modern totalitarian
states, unlike the liberal ones, had no intention of keeping the
treaties and in their hostility to the church went far beyond anything
that the most anti-clerical of her previous enemies had done.

The years of totalitarianism did much more, however, than teach
the church a bitter lesson. They also shattered the glasshouse in
which Catholics were supposed to live, protected from the surrounding world. There was really only a difference of degree in the rejection of the world as practised by Gregory XVI and by Pius IX.
Both deprived Catholics of their ability to fight for their faith and
to persevere under persecution. The only positive result of these
treaties was that the papacy managed to obtain important concessions enabling it to perfect, within the church, its own system of
absolute rule. Thus in the agreement on episcopal appointments
cardinal secretary of state Gasparri succeeded through remarkable
tenacity in getting the clause removed which required consultation
with the government concerned. The bishops therefore became
wholly dependent on Rome. This was at least more justifiable than
the nineteenth-century tendency to abolish the electoral rights of
cathedral chapters, but the present practice is certainly quite contrary to the decisions of the Council of Trent.

12 Catholic Action

Established by Leo XIII, Catholic Action received its final form under Pius X and Pius XI. It was intended as a movement to increase the role of the laity, but actually developed into an instrument of papal absolutism and as such placed the organisations of the laity, which in many countries enjoyed relative independence, under the hierarchy and papal control. Catholic Action also served as a means of making the church less political, which was the aim of Pius XI. It was supposed to organise Catholicism from within and in this way laid itself open to the fatal influence of integrism.

Concordats and Catholic Action therefore derive from one and the same state of mind. The concordats were to provide the Catholic church with special privileges and as far as this was possible to secure full religious dependence on Rome. Catholic Action was to imbue the religious sphere, separated as it had become from ordinary day-to-day affairs, with Catholic ideas. The movement perpetuated the old Vatican belief that it was possible to keep Catholics in a kind of limbo far away from the enticements of a wicked and hostile world. Such a sheltered existence was intended to add to the influence of the papacy and thus the movement matched the aims of the curia. But it also involved a greater burden of responsibilities which the Vatican was not always able to carry.

In countries with powerful Catholic organisations and in the Anglo-American Catholic world, Catholic Action met some reservations. Archbishop Pacelli, then papal nuncio in Germany, tried at the Magdeburg *Katholikentag* of 1928 to persuade German Catholics to accept it. The German Catholic organisations, however, were reluctant to surrender their relative independence vis à vis their own hierarchy. But in pastoral terms, Catholic Action (which Pius XII also fully supported) proved abortive. In some countries Catholics were preparing, through political parties and Christian trade unions, for the necessary adaptation to the modern world. But this process was fatally delayed through the creation by Catholic

Action of a Catholic political apartheid. The movement was developed in an Italian environment and exemplified the danger of transplanting such institutions to other countries. This did not prevent it from exerting a beneficial influence in countries such as Belgium, Holland or the United States where the independence of the church from the state facilitated the political activity of Catholics, or in the relatively primitive social conditions of south America where even a lay movement under clerical control could be considered an advance. In Italy and in Germany Catholic Action had an unsettling effect on existing Catholic organisations and contributed to their collapse under the pressure of fascism. This is also what happened to the German Centre Party which was weakened in its democratic stand by the effects of the encyclical *Quadragesimo anno,* as well as by the apolitical influence of Catholic Action. Another important factor was that Protestantism in Germany even exceeded Catholicism in hostility towards democracy and this situation practically led to the surrender of the state to the Nazi regime.

The German and Italian dictatorships presented Pius XII with problems that no other pope has been called on to face. His behaviour, in the years before and during the Second World War, presents today a picture of ambivalence. In one respect he was the pope par excellence who strove for perfection in everything. He raised his office to unprecedented spiritual heights. Never before had there been a pope who in his whole character, attitude and convictions, so obviously fulfilled the claim to be the Vicar of Christ. The inconsistency between his character and his actions during the Second World War, dictated as it was by various considerations, thus becomes all the more marked. But it is also proof of the radiating force of his personality that practically no one sensed this inconsistency in his lifetime.

His successor had the difficult task of breaking out of the circle. If John XXIII had been a pious simpleton like Pius X, as the curia

evidently assumed him to be, the papacy's dependence on its bureau-
cratic machinery would certainly have been increased, the gulf between papacy and the world widened, with added dangers for the
democratic development of the church. But John XXIII appealed
to the universality of Catholicism by inviting all the bishops of the
world to Rome to attend his Council. He freed himself from the
tutelage of the curia and opened the way for an entirely new development which was to be determined by the needs of the world
church rather than by the prejudices of Rome.

13 Relations between Italy and the Vatican 1922-63

The solution of the Roman question

Immediately after his election Pius XI did what both his predecessors had wanted to do but had been prevented from doing by the curia: he gave his blessing *urbi et orbi* from the balcony of St Peter's. He thereby indicated his resolve to end the pope's 'imprisonment' in Rome. Nevertheless another seven years passed before agreement with the Italian government was reached. Gasparri, whom Pius had inherited as secretary of state from Benedict XV, and Francesco Pacelli, a judge in the curia and a brother of Pope Pius XII, both played a decisive role in the tough negotiations. If this work of reconciliation could have been achieved by the new Italian Catholic party, an entirely new situation might have arisen for Italian democracy, but this was not to be. The *Partito Popolare* was still in its infancy and had never had any support from the Vatican, where its enemies included the cardinal secretary of state Gasparri. The hundred deputies of the party were, therefore, powerless to stop the destruction of Italian democracy. Right from the start the party was up against a fascist group with similar goals: opposition to the existing government, rejection of liberalism and socialism, support for the patriotic and nationalist ideal of Italian soldiers returned from the war. From its very beginning fascism found sympathisers also among the Italian clergy. And it was Mussolini who came to be credited with the great achievement of strengthening the foundations of the Italian state through reconciliation with the papacy. With the Lateran Treaty (11 February 1929) opposition to the more liberal Italian monarchy was increased and fascism thus opened a new era in Italian history. For loyal Catholics, too, there was now an outlet for their patriotism. Mussolini even found supporters among the higher Italian clergy who had so far reserved judgment. The Vatican derived considerable advantages from the concordat and from the financial agreements. The creation of the

Vatican City State met the demand for sovereignty. The transfer of state bonds to the value of 1,000 million lire and 750,000 million lire in notes, though considerably less than the Italian kingdom had offered in 1871, provided a sound basis for the papal exchequer. Catholicism became the established religion of Italy.

Two articles of the Lateran Treaty had a profound political effect. Members of the clergy and religious orders were forbidden to join or take part in any political movement. In exchange the Italian government undertook to support Catholic Action, provided it refrained from political activity. Some articles, such as the Catholic marriage legislation, were bitter pills for the fascists to swallow. In the chamber of deputies Mussolini therefore minimised the significance of his concessions to the Vatican, pointing out that what mattered more than the content of the treaties was the fact that agreement had been reached at all. His efforts were speedily vindicated in the overwhelming fascist victory in the elections of May 1929.

The rising tide of fascism

The Italian concordat had been signed by the Vatican in the belief that an advantageous settlement of this kind was worth the price of renouncing any special political influence on Italian politics. But this soon proved to be a delusion. Mussolini's return to the war of attrition, with its consequent irritations and persecutions, proved the unsoundness of the deal. Cardinal Gasparri, who was a well-known critic of the fascist regime, resigned on 7 February 1930 in an attempt to improve matters. The new cardinal secretary of state was the nuncio in Berlin, Eugenio Pacelli, but this change of office brought about no immediate improvement in the situation. In his encyclical *Non abbiamo bisogno* of 29 June 1931, at first suppressed in Italy and only published in Paris, Pius XI took issue with both the open and the disguised measures of oppression. However, his versatile secretary of state succeeded in preventing an open breach with the Italian government. Indeed, an agreement very favourable to Mussolini, with the Vatican meeting the fascist demands more than half-way, was reached on 7 September 1931 through the mediation of the Jesuit Tacchi Venturi. The Catholic organisations were preserved in name only, and associated with the fascist organisations in all secular activities. This was a surprising concession by the Vatican and it was not mitigated by the fact that the hierarchy retained control. Catholic organisations and Catholic Action were confined to the ecclesiastical domain. A further concession, as already mentioned, that went beyond the concordat was the ban on all political activities of the clergy.

The years up to 1937 were a time of apparent agreement which even extended to the adoption by the fascist state of certain theses of Catholic social teaching. The ideas about the corporate state developed by the encyclical *Quadragesimo anno,* published in 1931 on the fortieth anniversary of *Rerum novarum,* seemed to go far towards meeting fascist social policy. The corporate system which on 19 January 1939 replaced the party political structure of deputies seemed to put these ideas into practice. Mussolini formulated his aims on 10 November 1934 with reference to the ideal of social peace developed in *Quadragesimo anno*: 'We intend to create an organisation which within our society will slowly but surely iron out the differences between the highest and the lowest standards of living and will secure social justice'.

In effect this system meant that public life became less political and the dictatorship more dictatorial. The corporate order propagated by *Quadragesimo anno* was undoubtedly capable of an interpretation other than that which it received in Italy and Austria, but its anti-democratic tendency is unmistakable and explains why, in the nineteen-thirties, *Quadragesimo anno* was widely thought to stand for a new order that might help to overcome the frustrating party political system.

The links between Italy and the Vatican strengthened Italian illusions that the fascist state could be regarded as Catholic although Mussolini naturally gave priority to its fascist aspect when he said: 'The fascist state fully and wholly claims a moral character, it is Catholic but fascist, indeed above all, exclusively, essentially fascist'.

The fervent patriotism of the Italian clergy, especially of Pius XI and Pius XII, resulted in a general agreement between the Vatican and the policies of the Italian government, even on the war in Abyssinia. It was only because of the closer Italian alliance with Nazi Germany and the new emphasis on the pagan aspects of fascism that an estrangement came about which increased when Italy adopted racialist laws and came wholly under German domination. Pius XI had been enough of a realist to guard the church against too close a connection with Italian fascism. New conflicts arose towards the end of his pontificate; he was not prepared to give in to the state and would probably even have risked endangering the Lateran Treaty. The racialist laws were a clear breach of the concordat by which the Catholic marriage legislation had been declared binding for all Italians. In his view Italian racialism destroyed any possibility of an accord between the fascist government and Catholicism.

The relations between Italian fascism and Pius XII were marked from the outset by his efforts to save the peace, and when these failed, by his efforts to keep Italy out of the war. His attempts to interfere in his country's foreign affairs met with polite rebuttal. When Italy entered the war the Vatican became isolated and its diplomacy curtailed. Externally Pius XII maintained strict neutrality.

Post-war democracy in Italy

At the end of the war, Italy was in terrible political straits owing partly to the lack of democratic forces in the country. As in other liberated countries, the communists, who were the most consistent enemies of fascism, made tremendous progress. They began a ruthless campaign of revenge under the very eyes of the allied occupation powers, and new conflicts with the Vatican were inevitable. No political creed had ever been so consistently condemned by the Catholic church as communism. In his encyclical *Divini Redemptoris* of 19 March 1937, Pius XI had summarised all previous condemnations. It was obvious that a new democratic Italy could not arise from bourgeois Catholic co-operation with communist elements, except by invalidating the whole right-wing pattern of the 1929 reconciliation between the Vatican and the Italian government. The monarchy no longer mattered after the king's undignified escape in 1945 and after the defeat of fascism. Pius XII himself might have favoured the retention of the monarchy but he was unable to make a definite decision one way or the other. If he had spoken out for the monarchy, the referendum of 1946 might have produced different results. As it was, the monarchy was rejected by a majority of two million votes.

It was under the pressure of these circumstances that in 1943 the *Democrazia Cristiana,* as a movement of the Catholic middle classes, was already being formed by Alcide de Gasperi, former parliamentary chairman of the old *Partito Popolare.* De Gasperi had spent the years from 1929 to 1943 working in the Vatican library but had been careful to keep out of Vatican politics. In all this time he had never once crossed the threshold of the Vatican secretariat of state. He was adamant that Italian politics must not again be based on the unified organisation of Catholic Action because of its dependence on the curia and its emphatically apolitical nature. He wanted to

Pius XII with Luigi Gedda, the leader
of Italian Catholic Action. Gedda
played an important and controversial
role in Italian post-war politics.

construct the new Italian state on the model of the *Partito Popolare*
as a large middle-class part which, although Catholic, was to be
independent of the hierarchy and especially of the Vatican. Above
all he wanted to avoid embroiling the church in the party political
arena. De Gasperi's concept met from the start with the curia's
opposition. A party independent of the Vatican was quite contrary
to the authoritarian ideas of Pius XII, as the history of the following
years was to show. The Vatican wanted such a policy based on
Catholic principles to be carried out under the auspices of Catholic
Action, that is to say, under the hierarchy's watchful eyes. De
Gasperi's achievement was endangered more than once by the crises
arising from this disagreement. His opponent was Luigi Gedda,
the leader of Catholic Action, a man well versed in anti-democratic
intrigues, on whose counsels Pius XII relied for many years.

Gedda belonged to the extreme integrist school. Some of his
political views were extraordinarily naïve and resembled those of
Benigni. He once addressed a conference of the diocesan chairmen
of Catholic Action in these words:

Four centuries have passed since the laceration of Europe, which protestantism caused and under which we are still smarting. What has happened in
this time? Deterioration of conditions, the birth of socialism, at first only of
the romantic sort, but soon developing and turning into the political system of
communism. There you have the pernicious logic of error! From the distant
protestant revolution ushering in religious liberalism we can trace a direct line
via the political liberalism of the French Revolution to modern communism.
Today once more protestantism, initially barred from Italy, is on the move to
poison our nation with its side effects.

Such views were certainly unlikely to promote democracy in post-
war Italy.

Many clashes occurred between the other parties and Catholic
Action, which had Vatican elements behind it. Not infrequently these
also had the support of Pius XII. In 1952 Gedda attempted to put

pressure on De Gasperi through the so-called *Operazione Sturzo*.
In this he had the support of the Jesuit preacher Lombardi and undoubtedly acted with the pope's knowledge. His aim was to gather
all the right-wing parties from the *Democrazia Cristiana* to neo-
fascists and monarchists, and prevent a communist victory in the
communal elections. His scheme would have divided Italy into two
camps and destroyed Christian democracy as a popular force. For-
tunately the scheme failed because of Christian Democratic opposition. A remark by Monsignor Montini, as he then was, proves that
influential Vatican elements were at that time prepared to sacrifice
the Christian Democratic Party since it did not pursue exclusively
Catholic aims. Asked by Dr Emilio Bonomelli, the director of the
papal residence of Castel Gandolfo, whether the pope was aware that
these events would bring down the government, Montini is reported
to have replied: 'Isn't this precisely what you are aiming at? For a
long time you have said nothing else but that Christian Democracy
has ruined us and that Gedda and his Catholic Action are the only
effective force to take this party's place and fight communism!'

De Gasperi's greatest worry after this was that the Vatican's intervention might produce an anti-clerical tide in Italy by which his party would necessarily be isolated. Pius XII expressed himself 'greatly surprised' by the co-operation with the moderate socialists of Giuseppe Saragat which De Gasperi advocated in 1949 and the latter tried in a famous letter to explain his political aims: he wrote that the inter-denominational front which Gedda demanded was bound to lead to the setting up of a common anti-clerical front.

The pattern of the 1953 election campaign was repeated in 1957 when political conditions made the *apertura a sinistra,* as the alliance with the moderate socialists was called, inevitable. The anti-democratic right-wing parties of monarchists and neo-fascists and the liberals, who in Italy are wholly dependent on heavy industry, would have otherwise won the elections. Throughout Pius' reign the *apertura a sinistra* policy was opposed from many pulpits. Even the patriarch of Venice, cardinal Roncalli, was against it, although it was in his pontificate that the Vatican finally achieved political neutrality. But when he became pope, as John XXIII, Roncalli recognised that mere unbridled opposition to communism was an inadequate political programme for Italy.

It was he who inspired the attempt to move the church away from too close a commitment to the western world and on to a more neutral course in international affairs. In Italy this surprising change of front initially favoured the communists. But, on their side also, they were forced to look on the church as a power to be reckoned with. This change of policy proved a great advantage for the papacy. For the first time its outlook on the world and world affairs was no longer determined by the Italian political situation. The repercussions in Italy on the new policy towards communism were minimal. The papacy had finally freed itself from its involvement in Italian politics.

14 The papacy and the rest of the world 1918-63

Papal attempts at conciliation in France

The European resettlement after the First World War made France
once again the leading power on the continent, and thus restored
the pre-1870 conditions. The Vatican was gravely concerned that
the Treaty of Versailles would be detrimental to a genuine peace
settlement, but was nevertheless prepared to accept its provisions.
The Vatican's relations with France had been tense ever since the
law of separation of 1905, and it had become one of the first
diplomatic tasks of the Holy See to improve these relations.
Germany's passionate refusal to acknowledge that the war was lost
and that everything was changed had also to be reckoned with.
Church relations too, had to be established with the newly-founded
states.

In the political field the papacy was confronted by three factors:
communism, fascism and western democracy. Since communism
appeared to Rome as the epitome of godless idolatry, advances were
made towards the authoritarian regimes in the belief that they and
not the western democracies would more readily fight communism.
The political influence and significance of the papacy in world
affairs at that stage depended on its dealings with these political
forces which varied in every country. A climax was reached in 1937
when Pius XI issued pungent condemnations of communism and of
national socialism. But he never reached the conclusion in these two
declarations that he ought to come down positively on the side of
democracy.

While the legal position of the Catholic church in France was
still decided by the law of separation, the prestige of Catholicism
had been increased by the conduct of French Catholic priests during
the First World War and, helped by the skilful diplomacy of Benedict
XV, a more conciliatory atmosphere had been created. The appoint-
ment in 1919 of Monsignor Rémond as bishop in charge of the

occupied German territories was an agreeable surprise for the French government. Based on Mainz, Rémond even gained the approval of his German *confrères*.

This helped to improve relations with the French government. By the agreement of 12 February 1924 Pius XI, although refusing to recognise the anti-clerical legislation, did, however, agree to accept the guarantees offered by the French government for the associations of laymen to conserve the ownership of the church's property.

This reconciliation provoked the resistance of the integrist and conservative-monarchist forces in France which were still strongly represented in the French episcopate. Once again a basic dispute with the democratic republic threatened to endanger the unity of French Catholicism. Various declarations, especially those issued by cardinal Andrieu, archbishop of Bordeaux, against the 'godless government' marked the electoral campaign of 1924 and finally a Catholic Action Committee was set up. Attempts to drag the Vatican into this dispute were rejected by the nuncio in Paris. The result in the election of 11 May 1924 was a powerful anti-Catholic vote which produced a left-wing majority led by Edouard Herriot. In his government programme the new Prime Minister not only announced new measures against the Catholic church but also proposed the suppression of the French Embassy at the Vatican. This proposal passed the first chamber but was rejected by the senate. Only the speedy overthrow of Herriot on 10 April 1925 prevented a worsening of relations. A *modus vivendi* was reached on 4 December 1926 with a double treaty by which France also received the protectorate over Catholics living in its north African territories.

In the meantime a change occurred in the attitude of the French episcopate, for the defeat of 1924 was too blatant to be disregarded. In February 1924, shortly before the elections, some members of the episcopate, probably including archbishop Dubois of Paris, had issued an anonymous warning against attacking the anti-clerical laws. Their attitude was now fully vindicated. Rome was annoyed by the French integrists and pointedly rewarded the papal nuncio, archbishop Covetti, with the red hat.

The condemnation of the Action Française

The anti-democratic machinations originating within the *Action Française* enjoyed particularly strong support in the hierarchy. As I previously said, some of the writings of Charles Maurras, the leader of the movement, had been placed on the Index by Pius x in 1914, but this condemnation was not made known at the time since Maurras was regarded as a useful ally to the papacy in other ways. Pius xi devoted himself to a daily study of the *Action Française* press and finally decided to act. The immediate cause was an open letter, addressed to the Pope on 15 April 1926, which asked him to show greater consideration for the policy pursued by Pius x, and indeed, to ensure that his own successor would be a more loyal follower of Pius x than he was. At the same time, however, Rome was requested by cardinal Charost of Rennes to condemn the *Action Française*. In response to a question by the youth association of Bordeaux as to whether the *Action Française* could be considered as Catholic, cardinal Andrieu replied on 23 August 1926 that it could not. In the resulting conflict Pius xi intervened on 20 December 1926 with the publication of the condemnation signed by his predecessor. The pope emphasised that it was the religious views of Maurras, not his political views, to which objection had been taken. Maurras admired the Greek and Roman world for having subdued the Jewish and eastern element of Christianity. It seemed to him that an intransigent Catholicism allied with Auguste Comte's positivism and even with atheism stood for spiritual order as well as for the French national interest, whereas Jews, Deists and Protestants were relegated by him to the status of anarchists. He cherished the church for her civilising rather than her supernatural mission. Maurras' letter to the pope protesting against his condemnation remained unanswered.

The *Action Française* now openly revolted in France. In an article entitled *Non possumus,* it claimed that the condemnation was motivated by political considerations, abused the Holy Father in violent language and declared itself unable to pursue a papal rather than a French policy. The archbishops of Rouen, Bourges and Auch published Pius x's decree with some reluctance and reserve. Bishop Marty of Montauban even declared that he knew from reliable sources that no ban on the movement or its publications was intended by the pope, but this view was denied by the papal nuncio Maglione in his New Year's address of 7 January 1927; on 5 January 1927, Pius xi issued his own detailed condemnation of the writings and periodicals published by Maurras. The French hierarchy's reaction on 2 March was an address of submission drawn up by cardinal Luçon. However, some signatures were missing, among them those of bishop Marty, Monsignor de Llobel, coadjutor to the archbishop of Avignon, cardinal Coullié, archbishop of Lyons and bishop Penon, former bishop of Moulins. These prelates also refused to sign a further declaration of 8 March which carried the names of 119 bishops. All eventually submitted although their submissions did not always sound convincing. There was open rebellion among the professors of the French Seminary in Rome. After two official visits of inspection the rector, Le Floch, was deposed for having suppressed the decrees of the Holy Office and having incited his students against the papal decision. The Jesuit cardinal Billot, a former associate of Benigni, resigned in 1927. Continuous unrest among the French clergy necessitated further disciplinary measures. Finally the papal breve of 25 August 1929 again condemned the members of the *Action Française*.

This crisis was not entirely the end of French integrism. It raised its head once more among the French hierarchy when the ban was lifted by Pius XII on 10 July 1939, and it revived again in German-occupied France under the Pétain regime. But the way towards a peaceful settlement with the republic had been cleared. The financial provisions of 1929 made it possible for several exiled religious congregations and orders to return to France. A new era of friendship seemed to have opened with the state visit to the Vatican of the Prime Minister Pierre Laval. Laval resigned in 1936 and was followed by Léon Blum's popular front government which included communists. This greatly worried Pius XI, especially since a similar experiment made in Spain at the beginning of 1936 had produced the Spanish Civil War and the violent persecutions of the church. The events in France served as an occasion to issue the famous encyclical *Divini Redemptoris* of 19 March 1937 by which communism and the bolshevist system were once more condemned. But the popular front governments refrained from adding to the anti-church laws, and Vatican relations with France on the whole remained unimpaired. Pius XI, however, repeatedly deplored the indecisiveness of French policy towards Germany, which he regarded as symptomatic of the French democratic system.

The war years and after in France

On Pius XI's death, Europe was overshadowed by the threat of war. The Munich mood of euphoria had vanished. Those who still doubted Hitler's war-like intentions learned better on 16 March 1939 when German troops marched into Prague. Eugenio Pacelli, the new pope, a diplomat of the Roman school, was reputed to be sympathetic to Germany, but one of his first acts suggested that his sympathy did not extend to the Nazi regime. He appointed the former nuncio in Paris, Maglione, to be his cardinal secretary of state. It was due to Maglione's consistent attitude that the Maurras crisis had been terminated and followed by the church's reconciliation with France. Maglione knew and loved France; he was also a supporter of democracy, though familiar with its weaknesses. At that time the Vatican, more than any other government, clearly realised the dangers threatening Europe. The peace policy of Pius XII, in particular his proposal of May 1939 for a summit conference to help solve disputed questions, was inspired by his grave fear that the war which now seemed imminent would prove to be long and disastrous. Pius XII was unable to get any support for his proposals. Destiny took its course. Once hostilities had begun the pope's neutrality kept him in the background.

The defeat of France was a difficult test for the Vatican's relations with that country. Pius XII recognised the Pétain regime, but he also negotiated with De Gaulle who appointed a representative to the Holy See. After the evident failure of the Third Republic, events in France pointed clearly towards a solution on authoritarian lines. The Pétain-Laval government was not just an imitation of the fascist regimes. It had the backing, at least up to the German occupation in November 1942, of all the old conservative-authoritarian elements for whom the collapse of France had been but a confirmation of their views. Charles Maurras, with whose ideas Pétain had always sympathised, was among them. When on 10 July 1939 the newly elected pope lifted his predecessor's ban on the *Action Française,* this was bound to favour the conservative tendencies in the French hierarchy. But in supporting the Vichy regime as a Catholic-conservative solution for France, Catholic conservatism, which for almost a century had opposed any reconciliation between church and state, overshot the mark. The close collaboration between Vichy and the hierarchy was later regarded by the liberators and De Gaulle as an intolerable affront. They demanded that thirty-three of the collaborating bishops should be deposed. Pius XII was deeply shocked by the liberators' policy of ruthless revenge – it was said that about 100,000 Frenchmen were executed – and rejected the demand which he considered offended his position as head of the Catholic church. It was at this delicate moment that Angelo Roncalli presented his credentials as the new nuncio to De Gaulle on 7 January 1945. He was almost crushed between these two autocrats. He did not always follow the instructions of Pius XII and was at various times reproved for it. But his geniality and diplomatic skill generally prevailed in the end. Pius XII nominated him cardinal on 12 January 1953 and, according to the old custom which had been resumed, the French socialist president, Vincent Auriol, handed him the red biretta.

In 1946 France rid herself of De Gaulle's firm regime. A strong Catholic party, the *Mouvement républicain populaire* (MRP), which had developed in the Fourth Republic, produced some of the leading post-war politicians, such as Robert Schuman and Georges Bidault. It had the support of the powerful Christian trade unions. Reconciliation with the republic had finally been accomplished. Like the *Democrazia Cristiana* in Italy, the MRP was largely the product of the resistance movement. While its predecessor, the PDP *(Parti democrate populaire)* never achieved any real influence on the French political scene, the MRP by 1948 had become an important political factor with the support of some twenty-five to thirty per cent of the electorate. It was a movement with a passion for democracy and a markedly social programme that, unlike its Italian and German sister parties, carried out major reforms in social insurance, family allowances and the nationalised industries. The MRP soon encountered opposition by communists and gaullists and lost a good deal of ground in the nineteen-fifties when there was a swing to the right and its voting strength was reduced to between twelve and thirteen per cent. The MRP preserved the impulses it had originally derived from the social doctrines of the popes far longer than the Christian democrats in Italy and Germany. French Catholics had learned at last to come to terms with the separation of state and church and to make use of its advantages.

The Spanish Civil War

But while in France this separation, which was originally directed against the church, eventually turned in her favour, a similar experiment in Spain had catastrophic results.

After a troubled nineteenth century, Spain attained some stability in 1923 under the dictatorship of Primo de Rivera. There were close links between this regime and the church. Spanish Catholicism was endangered when Rivera fell in January 1930 and especially after the republican victory on 14 April 1931. The young Spanish republic did not disguise its hostility towards the church. The constitution of 9 December 1931 brought about, among other hostile measures, the separation of church and state by expropriating the church and abolishing religious instruction in schools. Pius XI protested against this on 3 June 1933, but as conditions were unlikely to improve, the pope gave his support to the founding of a Spanish party. This was a unique step in his pontificate and showed that he was well aware of the advantages to be derived in particular circumstances from the political representation of Catholics. In the spring of 1935 some hundred and twenty Catholic deputies joined the coalition government, on which they were represented by five ministers. They were unable to get the anti-church laws rescinded, but helped to bring about some improvement in the situation of the church. A chance majority vote led to the setting up of the popular front government in 1936 and to further measures against the church. With the assassination on 12 July 1936 of the monarchist leader Calvo Sotelo, the outbreak of the Civil War was inevitable, and in its course Catholics suffered cruel persecutions. Agreements were concluded on 7 June 1941 and 16 July 1946 with the victorious Franco regime which was well disposed towards the church. With the concordat of 27 August 1953 Catholicism was finally restored as the established religion of Spain with all the advantages of that position. In subsequent years there have been various occasions for tension between the Franco regime and the church, but conditions have become much more stable.

The Nazi rise to power

While the church thus suffered many setbacks in her dealings with the western liberal and social democracies, her situation in the post-First War German Republic seemed to be much more promising. This was due to the fact that the Catholic Centre Party had joined in the democratic efforts to build up the Weimar Republic and that its members occupied leading positions in all the cabinets from 1919 until 30 May 1932. Catholic co-operation was not always easy to obtain. The Weimar Republic was highly unpopular among the German middle classes, not least because it was dominated by the two political parties, the Social Democrats and the Centre Party which under Bismarck had been regarded as enemies of the national cause. Many members of the hierarchy, especially cardinal Faulhaber, archbishop of Munich, continued to cherish memories of the German monarchy. Repercussions of the unhappy dispute over Catholics joining non-denominational trade unions impeded the development of the Christian unions, although at times these had considerable influence over the policy of the Centre Party. That this party carried government responsibilities was, however, not sufficient to turn its own supporters into genuine democrats.

The efforts of Eugenio Pacelli, the papal nuncio in Munich, were concentrated almost from the beginning on reaching a concordat with the German Reich; in this he had the support of the conservative section of the Centre Party, especially of its leader, Monsignor

The signing of the concordat
with Hitler's Germany on 20 July 1933.
From left to right: Monsignor Kaas,
the leader of the now defunct Centre Party,
the German Vice-Chancellor Franz von
Papen, and Cardinal Pacelli, later Pius XII.

Kaas. However, nothing came of these efforts because of the hostile majority in the Reichstag. It was therefore decided to sign concordats with individual *Länder* such as Bavaria (1924), Prussia (1929) and Baden (1932).

Relations between the Catholic church and the new German democracy were ambiguous. The hierarchy encouraged Catholics to vote for the Centre Party, important positions in which were held by priests including, since 1928, the party chairmanship. On 10 February 1931 the bishops banned members of the Nazi party from receiving the sacraments, but this did not mean a commitment to democracy. The church's close involvement in German politics was regarded with great suspicion in Rome. Ideas about the corporate state, as developed in the encyclical *Quadragesimo anno,* were having their effect on Germany too and at a critical moment weakened the democratic substance of the Centre Party. One German Catholic who was particularly influenced by these ideas was Franz von Papen, who became chancellor on 1 June 1932. His authoritarian views contributed to the break-up of the Weimar Republic, and it was his support that enabled Hitler to take over as chancellor on 30 January 1933. After that the Vatican feared that the Catholic church might have to pay a heavy price for involving herself in German politics. Consequently Rome tried to play down the attitude of the German episcopate towards national socialism. An indirect, though friendly, reference to Hitler in the address which Pius XI gave to the consistory in March 1933 was due to this policy. The position of the Centre Party was already difficult enough, but the Roman attitude jeopardised it even more. On 23 March 1933 the Centre Party voted for the notorious Enabling Act by which the Weimar constitution was virtually abrogated. A few days later the German bishops withdrew their ban on Catholic membership of the Nazi movement. One fateful event led to another. Within weeks German political Catholicism had been annihilated.

The disastrous concordat of 1933

On 7 April 1933 Von Papen, now Hitler's vice-chancellor, arrived in Rome with a draft for a concordat couched in extremely favourable terms. With the pope's agreement, the cardinal secretary of state Pacelli increased the Roman demands hoping thereby to wreck the negotiations. But when even these conditions were accepted by Von Papen, no chance of backing out remained. The Vatican had already at the end of March indirectly expressed readiness for negotiations, and had thus from the outset undermined its own position. The concordat with Germany was signed on 20 July 1933.

No doubt the Vatican had some grounds for wanting a contractual settlement of this sort. As a result of the changes made by Hitler in the German constitution, the old *Länder* concordats had become practically worthless. Moreover, the Vatican was faced with the dissolution of the Centre Party and of the German Catholic organisations. But since the independence enjoyed both by this party and by the German Catholic associations had always been a constant

An die ehrwürdigen Brüder Erzbischöfe

und Bischöfe Deutschlands

und die anderen Oberhirten

die in Frieden und Gemeinschaft

mit dem Apostolischen Stuhle leben

über die Lage der katholischen Kirche im Deutschen Reich

Papst Pius XI.

Ehrwürdige Brüder
Gruß und Apostolischen Segen!

Mit brennender Sorge und steigendem Befremden beobachten Wir seit geraumer Zeit den Leidensweg der Kirche, die wachsende Bedrängnis der ihr in Gesinnung und Tat treubleibenden Bekenner und Bekennerinnen inmitten des Landes und des Volkes, dem St. Bonifatius einst die Licht- und Frohbotschaft von Christus und dem Reiche Gottes gebracht hat.

Diese Unsere Sorge ist nicht vermindert worden durch das, was die Uns an Unserem Krankenlager besuchenden Vertreter des hochwürdigsten Episkopats wahrheits- und pflichtgemäß berichtet haben. Neben viel Tröstlichem und Erhebendem aus dem Bekennerkampf ihrer Gläu-

The encyclical *Mit brennender Sorge* ('With burning anxiety') in which Pope Pius XI voiced his dismay at the increasing oppression of the church in Germany. The encyclical was secretly smuggled into Germany in March 1937. On Palm Sunday it was read from every Catholic pulpit throughout the country before a single copy of the document had fallen into the hands of the Nazis.

source of annoyance to Rome, their disappearance was not to be regretted in view of the unusually favourable legal settlement. In Germany, as in Italy, this attitude was soon to be proved fatally wrong. For Hitler it was a great political victory, at home and abroad, merely to have signed a treaty with the Vatican. It enabled him to destroy the last traces of political Catholicism in Germany, and it also proved his respectability in the eyes of the world. The Vatican tried from 1933 until 1937 to get Hitler to keep to his agreements, but in vain. The concordat provided for the possibility of such protests – the Nazi government would otherwise have regarded them as illegitimate interventions in German internal affairs – but it soon became obvious how fruitless they were. Against a world of enemies the church had nothing to hope from treaties but, as the Spanish example proved at that time, it had everything to gain from the realities of political representation.

At the end of 1936 the point had been reached when Rome had to surrender or continue the struggle with more effective weapons. Pius XI decided on the latter course. In the famous and sensational encyclical *Mit brennender Sorge,* issued on 14 March 1937, he unreservedly denounced the Nazi regime and its breaches of faith. The encyclical was drafted in German by cardinal Faulhaber of Munich. After that everyone in Germany expected total war against the church. At the conference of German bishops held at Fulda in May 1937, Count Preysing, the bishop of Berlin, proposed that the German hierarchy, too, should come out with a clear and emphatic condemnation of the Nazi regime, but this was prevented by cardinal Bertram, archbishop of Breslau, who was chairman of the conference. There was no bridging the gulf between the church and national socialism. The situation was then radically changed by Hitler's successes abroad, and by the foundation of Greater Germany including Austria and the Sudetenland. Any internal German opposition to Hitler became even more difficult.

The Austrian Chancellor Engelbert Dollfuss on his way to the *Michaelerkirche* in Vienna for a thanksgiving service after the unsuccessful Socialist revolution in February 1934. His victory over the social democrats was followed by the abolition of representative government and the creation of a Catholic corporate state in Austria. In July 1934 'the little Chancellor' was assassinated by the Nazis, whom he had opposed as bitterly as he had the socialists.

Austria 1918-38

In Austria after 1918 there had been initially a similar development to that in Germany. The new Austrian Republic also mainly relied on the support of social democrats and Catholics, but the difference was that these two parties were inveterately hostile to one another. Monsignor Ignaz Seipel, the astute leader of the Christian Social party, was federal chancellor several times from 1922 to 1929. He succeeded in bridging the political though not the ideological gap separating him from the socialists. Seipel was at first an opponent of the idea of the corporate state which his party had taken over from Von Vogelsang, but he later accepted it and in 1929 declared the Christian corporate state to be his real political goal. Seipel's views found an echo in the encyclical *Quadragesimo anno*.

On 20 May 1932 Engelbert Dollfuss took on the Austrian chancellorship, but his government had a parliamentary majority of only one vote. These circumstances and the fact that unlike Seipel, he was not the man to get along with socialists, forced Dollfuss towards a coup d'état. A formal error in a parliamentary vote on 4 March 1933 served as his excuse for eliminating the Vienna parliament altogether. His close links with the Catholic church were sealed on 5 June 1933 by a concordat that contained exceptionally favourable terms for the Vatican. A staunch opponent of the Austrian Nazi party, Dollfuss was urged on by Mussolini to settle accounts with the Austrian socialists who were defeated in the bloody street battles of February 1934. The new constitution of May 1934 abolished Austrian parliamentary democracy and set up a Christian corporate state.

Dollfuss' system was undoubtedly the most sincere of various attempts to give political expression to the ideas developed by *Quadragesimo anno*. It was, however, doomed to failure from the outset because of its frontal attack both on the Austrian left and

on the rising tide of national socialism. Dollfuss was assassinated on 25 July 1934 in an unsuccessful coup d'état of Austrian national socialists and his place was taken by Kurt von Schuschnigg who continued to expand the pattern of the corporate Austrian state. With growing pressure from right and left, relying mainly on the support of the 'Fatherland Front', a rallying movement of questionable political aims, the Schuschnigg regime grew increasingly fascist. In the eyes of their contemporaries, however, Catholic and fascist Italy, and Catholic and semi-fascist Austria were the two countries in which Catholic social and political concepts had found their most perfect expression.

The German occupation of Austria put an end to these experiments. The Austrian episcopate, led by cardinal Innitzer of Vienna, turned surprisingly quickly to Hitler, showing that the Schuschnigg regime had had little support even in the Catholic church. Cardinal Innitzer's undignified and enthusiastic declarations in favour of Hitler resulted in a summons to Rome where he was rebuked.

The papacy's appeasement of the Nazis

The frustrating effect of Roman centralisation on the national hierarchies could not have been more tellingly demonstrated than by these events. Since Rome was particularly sensitive to any independent moves by the German episcopate in case these might be interpreted by the Nazi regime as contravening the concordat, such moves did not take place. Roman protests against contraventions by the Nazi government were not merely ineffective, the Catholic faithful were not even told about them. The over-prudent, over-anxious attitude of the German episcopate in its turn produced a growing crisis of confidence among the Catholics who, the more loyal they felt towards the church, the less they were able to understand why their bishops behaved as they did. But the situation could be frustrating even for bishops. Cardinal Innitzer had been rebuked because in the name of the hierarchy he had appealed to Austrian Catholics to vote for Austria's union with the Third Reich. But when bishop Sproll of Rottenburg refused to participate in one of Hitler's plebiscites, he was not only banned from his diocese by the Nazis but also reprimanded by the Vatican for having endangered the German concordat. The German hierarchy and Pius XII were leaning over backwards in order to appease the Nazi regime, and their conduct became something of a scandal during the Second World War. There were protests from cardinal Faulhaber, from the evangelical bishop Wurm, and there was a memorable sermon preached in August 1941 by Count Galen, the bishop of Münster. These combined protests did have one effect: they stopped the mass extermination of the mentally ill which had begun in October 1939. However, the Catholic attitude towards the persecution of the Jews was far less clear. There was not a single protest by the German bishops or by Pius XII. The mass killing of Jews about which Pius XII was undoubtedly informed were mentioned only once in the correspondence between the German bishops and the pope and the effect of this passage is not entirely reassuring. In a letter dated 30 April 1943 Pius wrote to Count Preysing, bishop of Berlin:

The Holy See has in charity done what was in its power to do, both economically and morally, on behalf of Catholic non-Arians as well as believing Jews. It needed a maximum amount of patience and self-denial on the part of the executives of Our work of aid to meet the expectations, indeed demands of those who sought help and to master the diplomatic difficulties involved. We refrain from mentioning the very large sums in American currency which we have provided to enable emigrés to go overseas. We have given these sums gladly, for these people were in dire need; we have helped for the sake of divine reward and have not been seeking human gratitude. Nevertheless, Jewish organisations too have expressed their warmest appreciation for the Holy See's work of rescue.

In Our Christmas message we have referred to what is being done to non-Arians at the present time in the areas under German power. We have spoken briefly but we have been well understood. We have no need to emphasise that Our Fatherly love and care today especially goes out to those non-Arian or half-Arian Catholics, whose material existence has been destroyed and who are in a desperate spiritual plight; they are, as all others, sons and daughters of the church. But as the situation is at present we are unfortunately not able to help them effectively in other ways than by our prayers. But we are determined to raise our voice again on their behalf if this were necessary, circumstances permitting.[3]

The pope's silence, on the persecution of the Jews, has come to be regarded as a scandalous blot on an otherwise impressive pontificate. The official documents so far published suggest that Pius XII considered a public protest to be useless on the grounds that he would be unable to change matters and because he feared that he might cause a grave crisis of conscience among German Catholics. But Pius also feared, careful and anxious diplomat that he was, that a public accusation of this kind would be fatal to his neutrality. Up to the very end Pius considered Soviet Russia to be the real danger to Europe, and had hopes of bringing about a peace settlement which would save the east European nations from Bolshevism. For this reason he avoided everything that might have caused a breach with Germany. This attitude certainly sprang from his basic conservative outlook which knew no greater evil than communism. It was also evident to Pius that while no mediation of his would delay the final collapse of the Nazi regime the Soviet occupation of central Europe was an event that would be irrevocable.

His attitude was certainly open to many objections, and above all to the question whether a course of action so exclusively determined by tactical considerations is appropriate for the representative of Christ on earth, however suitable it may seem for the administrative head of the Catholic church. But we cannot accept the primitive and one-sided condemnation of this pope which is the message of Rolf Hochhuth's drama *The Representative,* even though we may agree with the author's contention that Pius XII failed when he was faced with responsibilities that were beyond a single individual's capacity. However, the attempts made by the Vatican after 1945 to conceal the truth weigh more heavily against the pope than his understandable human failure. At that time an open explanation of the reasons that lay behind his conduct would have been widely welcomed. But Pius XII never publicly voiced any regret or explanation, acting indeed as though there had never been any collaboration with fascism or any special consideration shown towards the Nazi regime.

Post-war Germany

It was, however, Pius XII who after the collapse of Germany found the first words of encouragement for the German people. In 1946 bishop Preysing of Berlin, the pope's trusted friend, and bishop Galen of Münster were rewarded with the red hat for their courageous conduct during the Third Reich. Germany as in 1918 received papal succour in the form of food and clothing. A political party inspired by Christian precepts was formed after 1945, as in both France and Italy. When the German Federal Republic was set up in 1949, the Christian Democratic Union (CDU) – called in Bavaria the Christian Social Union (CSU) – formed a government, and from 1957 till 1961 commanded an absolute majority in the Bonn parliament. The CDU, like its French and Italian sister parties, emphasised its non-denominational character. The so-called 'Ahlener Programme', initially a progressive social policy, has since been replaced by one appealing mainly to conservative and middle-class interests and important parts of papal social teaching have been dropped in the process.

The validity of the German concordat on which doubts had been cast was reaffirmed in 1957 by an important judgment of the newly created Federal Constitutional Court. Essential parts of this agreement, however, are no longer in force owing to the federal constitution of the new West German state. In the eastern parts of Germany, occupied by the Soviet Union, it became impossible to enforce the validity of the concordat, and the church continues to be exposed to various forms of oppression.

Persecution of Catholics in eastern Europe

The position of the church in eastern Europe after 1918 is characterised by two phases. One was the bourgeois-liberal era in which the church in some countries clashed with nationalist forces and suffered persecutions on account of her long-established links with the German and Austrian monarchies. This was followed by the era of persecution which began in 1939.

In Poland, Catholicism had always derived advantages from the fact that the church had been an important element of national unity

Cardinal Hlond, (1881–1948) primate of Poland, at the Eucharistic Congress of 1934 in Brazil. He fled to Rome after the German invasion of Poland in 1939, went to France in 1940 and was imprisoned by the Germans from 1944 to 1945. In 1946 he returned to Poland as archbishop of Warsaw and faced the attack by the Polish communist regime on the Catholic church.

throughout nearly a century and a half of Russian, Prussian and Austrian foreign rule and enjoyed the support of a large section of the middle classes. Shortly after Poland had regained her independence in 1918, it was Achille Ratti, later Pius XI, who, on a special diplomatic mission, settled the problems of the new geographical pattern of the church, and prepared for the concordat of 1925.

Between 1925 and 1939 the hierarchy played an important role in Polish politics, which was terminated by the catastrophic invasion of 1939. In those parts of Poland occupied by the Soviet Union the church was totally suppressed; in the German-occupied parts a terror regime was launched and some twenty per cent of the Polish clergy were among its victims. Attempts by the Vatican to improve the lot of Polish Catholics were in vain. Germany rejected all representations, arguing that the German concordat did not extend to the Polish areas. The inhuman conditions in Poland under the Nazi occupation are revealed in the correspondence of Pius XII and the Polish bishops from 1939 to 1945.

Cardinal Hlond, the Polish primate, who had escaped to Rome in 1939, fell into German hands in France in 1940 and was interned in Germany. He returned to Poland on 20 July 1945 with papal authority to reorganise the Polish church. Apostolic administrators had already been appointed on 18 May 1945 for the Polish-occupied, former German dioceses of Breslau, Oppeln, Allenstein, Landsberg and Danzig. On 12 September 1945 the Polish government revoked the concordat of 1925. A systematic persecution of the church began which reached its climax with the arrest and imprisonment of the then primate of Poland, archbishop Wyszynski, who was in prison until 1956. In 1957 he was allowed to go to Rome to receive the red hat from the pope. One of the reasons for the persecution of the church by the Polish communist government was the condemnation of communism which the Holy Office had issued on 1 July 1949. This attempt to erect a barrier between Catholics and their com-

munist masters was bound to have dreadful consequences, as the treatment of the church in Czechoslovakia, Hungary, Rumania and Yugoslavia also shows. The Vatican decree, of course, served too as a useful pretext for settling old scores with bourgeois enemies. The evident partisanship of the church in favour of the Hungarian rebellion of 1956 once more created great difficulties for Catholics in eastern Europe, until the post-Stalinist era paved the way for more settled relations.

It was only under John XXIII that a new phase began for the church in the communist world. On 7 March 1963, a few months before the pope's death. Khrushchev's son-in-law Adzhubay was received in the Vatican. This was an unprecedented event. Five weeks later the encyclical *Pacem in terris* was published which, while upholding the condemnation of communism, emphasised the necessity of peaceful co-existence. John XXIII endeavoured to work for positive goals even though these could only be dimly foreseen and it was this that constituted the most important and revolutionary impact of his

An. et vol. LIII   15 Iulii 1961   (Ser. III, v. III) - N. 8

ACTA APOSTOLICAE SEDIS

COMMENTARIUM OFFICIALE

Directio: Palazzo Apostolico – Città del Vaticano — *Administratio:* Libreria Editrice Vaticana

ACTA IOANNIS PP. XXIII

LITTERAE ENCYCLICAE

Ad Venerabiles Fratres Patriarchas, Primates, Archiepiscopos, Episcopos aliosque locorum Ordinarios, pacem et communionem cum Apostolica Sede habentes, itemque ad universum clerum et christifideles catholici orbis: de recentioribus rerum socialium processibus ad christiana praecepta componendis.

IOANNES PP. XXIII

VENERABILES FRATRES, DILECTI FILII
SALUTEM ET APOSTOLICAM BENEDICTIONEM

MATER ET MAGISTRA gentium a Christo Iesu ob eam causam catholica Ecclesia constituta est, ut, per saeculorum decursum, omnes, qui in eius sinum et amplexum venturi essent, cum praestantioris vitae plenitudine salutem reperirent. Cui quidem Ecclesiae, *columnae et firmamento veritatis*,[1] duplex illud sanctissimus eius Conditor munus detulit, ut sibi pareret filios, et, quos peperisset, doceret et regeret, materna consulens providentia sive singulorum hominum sive populorum vitae, cuius excellentem dignitatem ipsa summo semper in honore habuit, vigilanterque tuita est.

---

[1] Cfr. *I Tim.* III, 15.

Left First page of the encyclical *Mater et Magistra* (issued on the seventieth anniversary of *Rerum novarum*) which anticipated the decisions of Vatican II and defined the new relationship of Catholicism to the temporal order. *Below* John F. Kennedy, the first Catholic President of the United Sates, is received at the Vatican by Paul VI

pontificate. A significant discussion has since begun among Italian, French and even Polish communists as to whether marxist atheism should be seen as an integral part of the communist creed or as a time-bound nineteenth-century factor of only tactical significance and thus to be dispensed with if necessary. While it is unlikely that the Catholic church will move on to more intimate terms with the communist system, she has at least broken through her rigid anti-communist attitude which prevailed from 1922 to 1963.

The papacy and the United States

It was this attitude that helped after 1945 to drive the church into the American camp. For a long time Rome had found it exceedingly difficult to establish a good relationship with the United States. American Protestant prejudice still played a role in the presidential elections of 1928 and brought about the defeat of Alfred E. Smith, the first Catholic to stand for this office. Protestant prejudice was at the bottom of American support for the persecution of the church in Mexico under the then communist regime. Pacelli's visit to the United States in 1936 helped to improve the situation. A closer contact was developed and at the time of the Second Vatican Council it was said of the American episcopate that it was a perfect mirror of the thinking, aims and indeed prejudices of the Roman curia. Diplomatic relations were established in 1941 although only in the form of a personal mission by the American diplomat Myron C. Taylor. The unconventional letter by which President Roosevelt announced Taylor's arrival caused astonishment in the protocol-conscious Vatican. Roosevelt described himself as the pope's 'sincere good friend' and ended with 'most cordially yours', but this did set the seal on an increasingly friendly relationship. After 1948 the rigid American Catholic anti-communist line found a typical expression in such prominent figures as cardinal Spellman and the Catholic senator Joe McCarthy. Catholicism in the United States, as also in Europe, acquired the dangerous reputation of providing the most reliable protagonists in the cold war. In the United States this trend was overcome when John F. Kennedy became the first American Catholic president. It was Kennedy who inspired John XXIII's vision of future contact with the communist world, although as patriarch of Venice he had opposed this. In his encyclical *Mater et Magistra* John XXIII made a clear and unequivocal pronouncement in favour of democracy and of a social order based on freedom.

15 Towards the Vatican Council

The Catholic intellectual situation at the beginning of the nineteen-twenties was not unlike that of the early nineteenth century. As the upheavals of the French Revolution had then proved an impossible burden for the Catholic reform movement and had rendered it incapable of exerting a formative influence, so now it was the after-effects of the modernist conflict which prevented the intellectual reform of the papacy. The attempt to erect an exclusively Catholic system based on the concordats, on the political and social teaching of Leo XIII and on Catholic Action, lacked the necessary theological basis. In the modernist conflict the papacy had rejected any reconciliation between modern learning and theology. While they suppressed some excesses of this resistance against the modern world, Benedict XV and Pius XI were far from compromising on the basic decision against any intellectual confrontation with new ideas. Indeed, it was held, as it had been since the eighteenth century, that the totality of Catholic belief made any intellectual dealings with current ideas unnecessary.

But the decision against any reconciliation of theology with science was bound to weaken with the disintegration of the sheltered Catholic existence and the growing power of science and scientific method in the modern world. It was in this respect, quite apart from the political developments, that the papacy was bound to be the loser. The dominating personalities of Pius XI and Pius XII prevented most people from being aware of the possibility of change until Pius XII's death. The exclusiveness of the Catholic system was deliberately emphasised under Pius XI. He took up the old tradition of celebrating papal jubilees as a means of enhancing the pope's position. As the history of the past hundred and fifty years had shown, these popular links strengthened the papacy's isolation from the trends of the times. Following the practice established by Pius IX, Pius XI celebrated in 1929 the golden jubilee of his priesthood and decreed that the nineteen-hundredth anniversary of the death of Christ in 1933 should be kept as a Holy Year. After 1922, international eucharistic congresses were held every two years in spectacular style, the pope appointing special cardinal legates and after 1931 addressing the crowds with personal messages broadcast on Vatican Radio which had been inaugurated in that year.

The authoritarianism of Pius XI and XII

The style of government of Pius XI resembled that of a great spiritual potentate. In his encyclicals, especially in those dealing with pastoral matters, he laid down general rules to be followed by Catholics; his precepts were authoritarian in character. In the encyclical on marriage, *Casti connubii* of 31 December 1930, procreation was stated to be the primary and essential purpose of matrimony. In the encyclical on the education of youth, *Divini illius Magistri* of 31 December 1929, co-educational as well as inter-denominational schools were banned for Catholics. While these encyclicals were part of the process of shielding Catholics from worldly contamination, they nevertheless started a dangerous practice that led to increased regimentation and they also increased the pope's enthusiasm for making authoritarian pronouncements on all kinds of pastoral questions. This was of course what the curia, who would have liked a decisive say in all important pastoral questions, wanted but the capacities of papal rule, based exclusively as it was on the will of one man, were certainly overtaxed.

The limitations of the curial approach were obvious, but it had certain advantages in matters of wider church administration. Pius XI and Pius XII showed themselves particularly far-sighted in promoting a missionary policy based on the native clergy. In the encyclical *Rerum ecclesiae* of 28 February 1926, Pius XI prepared the ground for the de-westernisation of Catholic missions. Pius XII continued this policy and thereby saved the church from setbacks in the missionary areas, when, after the Second World War, western colonialism was on the way out. But all attempts to establish closer relations with other denominations failed. This was not least because Rome in its over-simplified black and white approach lacked the perception to recognise the special theological traditions of other Christian churches. Caught up in its own administrative and technical style of church government, Rome could only envisage the restoration of Christian unity (which Pius XI made one of his aims) as the repentant return of prodigal sons to the forgiving bosom of the Catholic church. Discussions on Christian reunion sponsored by the Belgian cardinal Mercier and by Lord Halifax took place between 1921 and 1925 at Malines in Belgium but they had no chance of success. Pius XII rejected the official participation of the Catholic church in ecumenical gatherings on the same grounds. Rome was absolutely incapable of realising that the necessary conditions for any discussion on Christian unity were absent, owing to its own narrow theological approach which was founded on neoscholasticism and the rejection of modern religious thought.

It was in theology in particular that the Roman church became even more alienated from the common Christian basis. Above all there were the advances in mariology, always greatly cherished by the Catholic church, and so especially linked with the rise of the papacy. The proclamation of the dogma of the Immaculate Conception in 1854 marked an important stage on the road to papal absolutism and infallibility. Henceforth, the curia developed a particularly extreme form of marian devotions which received further emphasis through the apparitions of Lourdes (1858) and Fatima (1917), though the latter was only recognised by the Vatican in 1930 after a searching investigation. Pius XII who in 1942 consecrated the whole world to the Immaculate Heart of Mary was particularly attached to Fatima with its messages that had been communicated only to the pope. The proclamation on 1 November 1950 of the dogma of the bodily assumption of Mary into heaven was the climax of these marian trends. In the last years of the reign of Pius XII Roman Catholic mariology came dangerously close to mariolatry. Pius XI had been much more restrained in this respect, though by introducing the feast of Christ the King in 1925 and by linking it with the consecration of the world to the most Sacred Heart of Jesus, he developed another devotional ideal that was particularly characteristic of him.

Another controversial theological decision by Pius XII was proclaimed not *ex cathedra,* that is, infallibly, but had all the weight of his authority behind it and was thus not to be lightly set aside. This was contained in the encyclical *Mystici corporis Christi* of 29 June 1943 and concerned the interpretation of the church as the mystical body of Christ. His thesis was only partly reaffirmed by the Second Vatican Council.

There were times when it seemed as though Pius XII would take up the theological ideas which had emerged at the end of the Second World War, particularly in France. They were connected with the special conditions of the European resistance movements and stressed the necessity of making the church more receptive towards the world. A first indication was the letter *Divini afflante spiritu* of 30 September 1943 by which Catholic biblical scholars were finally granted the freedom of enquiry which they needed. This important instruction was supplemented on 16 January 1948 by a letter of the papal biblical commission, addressed to cardinal Suhard of Paris which closely approached the new theological thinking. On 20 November 1947 Pius XII issued his encyclical *Mediator Dei* on the liturgy in which he reaffirmed and encouraged the liturgical reforms that had been initiated in the nineteen-twenties in Austria and Germany, especially by Pius Parsch and Romano Guardini. But the Holy Year of 1950 saw the end of this new liberation and ushered in the conservatism of the latter part of

Pius XII's pontificate. Facing the hundred thousand pilgrims who, for the first time in his reign, had come to Rome, Pius missed a great opportunity to clarify his own stand on national socialism and the persecutions of the Jews or indeed to show, as many had hoped he would, his receptiveness for the *théologie nouvelle*. The French experiment of the worker-priests, encouraged by cardinal Suhard, had stirred the whole world. It was expected that Rome would support this new attitude in the church.

But Pius XII could not bring himself to decide in its favour. It was not that he disregarded, as had Pius X, the necessity of opening up the church towards modern thinking: his later utterances show that he was well aware of this need. But he feared that things would get out of hand if he supported the new trends. He therefore pronounced against them on three important occasions: through the proclamation of the dogma of the Assumption, by taking up the cause for the beatification of Pius IX, and in 1951 by the beatification of Pius X. This was a deliberate move in favour of the two popes who had been the most emphatic advocates of the church's retreat from an encroaching world of science, politics and autonomous human development. The third and not least important occasion was the publication on 12 August 1950 of the encyclical *Humani generis* which named and rejected the new trends: existentialism, historicism, the false theory of evolution, the urge for innovations, the Catholic feeling of inferiority with regard to modern science, the tendency to minimise the differences between the churches, the importance of theological concepts, etc. The encyclical started a kind of neo-modernist persecution. Amongst its victims were Yves Congar and Teilhard de Chardin, the two outstanding Catholic minds of that time. This development was not entirely unexpected for Pius XII had foreshadowed it in some addresses which he gave in 1946. The real purpose of the encyclical was clearly stated in its title: 'Concerning certain false opinions that threaten to undermine the bases of Catholic teaching'. Soon the emphasis throughout the church was on conservatism. On 23 August 1953 cardinal Feltin was ordered by the nuncio Marella, Roncalli's successor in Paris, to close the *Mission de Paris* and end the worker-priest experiment. The canonisation of Pius X, enacted with great solemnity in 1954, came as a renewed confirmation of the conservative trend.

The absolutist rule of Pius XII

There was no repetition, however, after 1950 of the events under Pius X; this was due to the wholly different personality of Pius XII. He was not the man to leave the field to the curia's heresy-hunters as had been done during the modernist and integrist conflicts. A highly educated and sensitive man, not entirely free from intellectual arrogance and personal vanity, Pius refused to be influenced by the apparatus of the curia from which he himself had arisen and which he knew only too well. He developed his own way of running the church. Important positions in the curia, such as the secretariat of state, had been left vacant after the death of cardinal Maglione in 1934. Pius wanted, as he often said 'not collaborators but executors'. Under him papal absolutism reached its ultimate heights. He ruled the church with the help of a small staff into which towards the end of his life corrupt and unworthy elements had insinuated themselves. With his ascetic looks and majestic gestures Pius XII seemed the very incarnation of the papacy to his contemporaries, Catholic and non-Catholic alike.

In his innumerable addresses he pronounced on a great variety of subjects. In a very typical over-estimation of his papal office he regarded these addresses not as contributions for discussion but as utterances of a binding nature for Catholics. As he put it in *Humani generis,* 'When the popes explicitly pronounce judgment on a hitherto controversial question, it is a clear indication to all of us that, according to the intention and will of the popes, it should no longer be subject to free discussion by theologians'. The addresses of Pius XII therefore evoked no discussion inside the church, nor, thoughtful as they were, and in retrospect sometimes even prophetic, did they have any influence. When he died, the Catholic church found herself in the same fossilised state as she had been at the death of Leo XIII.

Humble beginning of John XIII

At first the curia's view of the devout John XXIII as a second Pius X was by no means unjustifiable. In the first years of his pontificate, up to the opening of the Second Vatican Council in 1962, he was almost helplessly at the mercy of his curial advisors. Having filled the most important offices with his nominees, he gave the reins to the curia in a manner unthinkable under Pius XII. His way of ruling indeed seemed ambiguous at first. Some of his spontaneous, warm-hearted gestures and actions were opposed by other apparently contradictory ones. Even in his talk with his secretary of state of 20 January 1959, when he outlined what were to be the three goals of his pontificate: a Roman diocesan synod, a general council of the church and the reform of canon law, the breakthrough was by no means in sight. The Roman synod of January 1960 was held without any public debate and recalled the dictatorial procedure of the First Vatican Council. Some of the decisions which were issued by the Holy Office in subsequent months confirmed these growing suspicions. On 3 July 1959, for example, the Holy Office decided, against all the representations of cardinal Feltin, that the French worker-priests must be replaced by laymen. When the Holy Office issued a new warning to New Testament scholars (20 June 1961), praised the advantages of Latin for keeping the faith free from error (22 February 1962), and warned against theological interpretations of the work of Teilhard de Chardin (30 June 1962), all

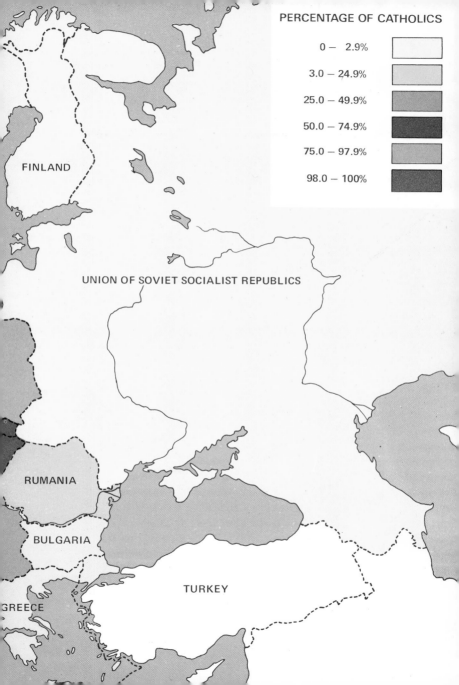

PERCENTAGE OF CATHOLICS

0 — 2.9%

3.0 — 24.9%

25.0 — 49.9%

50.0 — 74.9%

75.0 — 97.9%

98.0 — 100%

FINLAND

UNION OF SOVIET SOCIALIST REPUBLICS

RUMANIA

BULGARIA

TURKEY

GREECE

Cardinal Roncalli, later Pope John XXIII, achieved a diplomatic
triumph as nuncio in Paris after the Second World War
by preventing the deposition of thirty-three French bishops accused
of collaboration by General de Gaulle. This photograph taken
outside a Paris church with worker-priests illustrates the simplicity
and humanity of his approach to children, to the humble and the poor.

these measures seemed but to point in the same reactionary direction. The first preparations and the *schemata* drawn up for the
Council also suggested a regressive tendency, almost a relapse into
reactionary practices even beyond those of Pius XII. Only the encyclical *Mater et Magistra* of 15 May 1961, which I shall discuss
separately, shows a different spirit.

Yet, it was due to John XXIII that the Vatican Council finally
became the unique and most liberating event in the twentieth-century
Catholic church so far, although not in the way usually understood.
It is true that he was personally responsible for many innovations;
the Vatican, for instance, lost much of its severe rigidity, and his
own personal utterances awakened hopes of change. But the doubts
were by no means removed by the time the Council opened. When
so much emphasis is placed nowadays on the revolutionary aspects
of the reign of John XXIII, it is frequently forgotten that *Papa
Giovanni* himself was anything but a revolutionary. His great achievement, however, by means of the Council, was to have given modern
theology a fair chance against the curia. He was not likely to reform
the church through his own superior theological vision, for his
whole upbringing made him ill-equipped for such a task. But when
he invited the Fathers of the church to Rome he knew what he was
doing. Although the curia had managed to provide him with a good
deal of false or one-sided information in the first years of his pontificate, these restrictions on his position merely convinced John of
the absolute necessity of cutting across the stuffy Roman atmosphere. The only solution as far as he was concerned was to invite
the bishops and with them the needs and concerns of the whole
world church to Rome. His own career had taught him that the
curial style of government and its denial of all modern influences
was not necessarily the only possible one. As a young man, secretary
to the gifted and for him exemplary bishop Radini Tedeschi, he had
been denounced by the Holy Office for his connections with moder-

nists. Later he himself worked for some years in the curia, and in 1925 was appointed apostolic visitor to Bulgaria. In 1934 he became apostolic delegate to Turkey and Greece, and for ten years maintained the closest links with the eastern churches. But even more important for his future career was the Paris nunciature which he began on 23 December 1944. Pius XII nominated him cardinal on 12 January 1953, while he was still nuncio, and patriarch of Venice three days later. From 1952 he had also acted as permanent Vatican observer to UNESCO.

In those years in Paris, Angelo Roncalli had a chance of observing closely cardinal Suhard's worker-priest experiment and studying the background of the new Catholic ideas that aimed at greater balance and at realising the church's duty of being a leavening influence in the world. Roncalli, therefore, knew perfectly well who the men were who would be making themselves heard at the Council. In his famous opening speech of 11 October 1962 he addressed the rising new forces in the church with encouragement. It was thus no surprise to him when, on 13 October, in St Peter's, cardinal Liénart of Lille, the second-oldest of the cardinals, got to his feet to propose, amid loud applause from the Council Fathers, that the electoral lists for membership of particular commissions – which bore the reactionary imprint of their curial authors – be discarded and that the elections be postponed for a few days until the Council Fathers had been able to get to know each other better. It was then that the miracle of the Council was firmly set on its course and John XXIII's hopes for a change in the church's attitude to the world began to seem near fulfilment. He was now able to sit back and await further developments.

The influences behind the Council

What happened in the Council after that has a long history; and undoubtedly it is one of the most exciting chapters in the history of ideas in the western world. It is the as yet unrecorded story of modern Catholic theology. Here we can trace it in its essential outlines only, but these suggest that the 'miracle' of the Council was in fact the product of a much older intellectual development which confirms, more convincingly than anything else, that the church is truly the Church of Jesus Christ.

We shall have to go back to the beginnings of the modernist dispute. The pontificate of Leo XIII was certainly most receptive both to the world and to learning, but in the theological field it created a situation which the curia was unable to match intellectually in any comparable way. The fate of Alfred Loisy and his friend Von Hügel may help to illustrate what happened. Von Hügel continued to maintain friendly links between the church and both his excommunicated friends, Loisy and Tyrrell. It was due to him that, through bitterness over their disgraceful treatment, they did not turn into enemies of the church, although Rome persisted in seeing them as such. Von Hügel had become convinced that the church must share in the events of the age. He was passionately opposed to all restrictions of thought and research and tried, if only for the sake of saving the church's intellectual prestige, to keep his friends within the fold. In a letter of 9 December 1921 addressed to his niece Gwendoline Plunket Greene, he wrote:

As to myself, I find myself inclined to be very zealous to help souls to make the most of what they already have . . . And again, to do all I can to make the old church as inhabitable *intellectually* as ever I can – not because the intellect is the most important thing in religion – it is not; but because the old church already possesses in full the knowledge and the aids to *spirituality*, whilst, for various reasons which would fill a volume, it is much less strong as regards the needs, rights and duties of the mental life. Thus my second zeal includes the ardent wish and hope of serving sore and sulky, fallen-off or falling-off R.C.s – to heal their wounds and bring them back. *One* fallen R.C. gives me more pain than a *hundred* accessions to the church give me joy. For it is the *sticking it* which really matters and which is difficult.[4]

Loisy and Tyrrell were initially moved by very similar considerations. They wanted to demonstrate that it was possible for Catholics to deal critically with the results of modern science and especially with the philological methods of Protestant bible criticism. It was a tremendous blow to them when the Roman condemnations and the whole modernist hysteria showed that the unreserved search for truth as applied to the studies of scripture was impossible within Catholicism. But even after his condemnation Loisy's writings continued to influence Catholic theologians, particularly those born at the beginning of the century who became the initiators of the new theology. The 'Congress for the history of Christianity' held in Paris in 1927 on the occasion of Loisy's seventieth birthday was an important stage also on the road of modern Catholic biblical scholarship. Although Loisy died unreconciled with the Catholic church, he nevertheless felt that he belonged to her and his work has always remained part of Catholic thinking.

In the conflicts over Loisy during the modernist and integrist crises Rome took up an extreme position that was quite untenable, for it implied that any application of modern methods of scholarship in theology was necessarily heresy. This kind of extremism must ultimately put an end to all discussion. But Rome was prepared neither to admit to having been wrong about modernism nor, perhaps from a certain feeling of shame, to continue the persecutions with the original impetus. This does not mean that no condemnations occurred in the nineteen-twenties and thirties. One of the most outrageous cases was that of the German Catholic priest-writer and theologian Joseph Wittig. He came into conflict with the church authorities over an article published in 1922 in the review *Hochland* in which he contrasted what he described as 'God's revelation incarnated in man' with the rigid, conceptual, legalistic approach of contemporary theology. He was promptly suspended from his university professorship at Breslau and excommunicated in 1926; he later married and in 1946 was reconciled with the church, but without any satisfactory explanation being given. His case is only too typical of a whole series of condemnations by the Holy Office that were carried out arbitrarily and without the defendants having any opportunity of explaining their position.

Rome's failure to suppress the new theology

After 1922 the atmosphere for new thought improved and attempts to find a synthesis between Catholicism and the world developed slowly like a smouldering fire. Spectacular clashes were avoided by the Roman authorities who behaved with moderate tolerance, intervening only where this was thought to be absolutely necessary. *Humani generis* (1950) and the subsequent neo-modernist persecution mark the point where the slow fire threatened to become an open conflagration. Some of it was suppressed once more; but everything was already moving towards the decisions of the Council and certain developments could no longer be hindered.

Loisy's German counterpart was Hermann Schell, whose *Christus, das Evangelium und seine weltgeschichtliche Bedeutung* ('Christ, the gospel and its historical significance') (1903), had far-reaching and fruitful effects against which attempts at suppression were useless. Friedrich Wilhelm Maier was another of the German scholars who initiated the break-through from the anti-modernist phase to the Second Vatican Council. His commentary on the first three, or synoptic, gospels and his by no means uncritical usage of the Protestant two-document-hypothesis (that is, that Mark was written first, and was copied by Matthew and Luke) caused this book to be put on the Index in 1912; he was disciplined, but later from 1945-7 became an eminent professor of New Testament exegesis in Munich. More widely known in Germany and beyond were the writings on literary, liturgical, theological and philosophical subjects of Romano Guardini (1886-1968). He was professor 'for the philosophy of religion and the Catholic world view' *(Weltanschauung)*, a university chair which had been specially created for him in 1923 in Berlin. Guardini laid the foundations for the liturgical reforms, which the Second Vatican Council enacted forty years later, and indeed prepared for a complete new Catholic intellectual approach to the problems of man in the technological world of the twentieth century. In France Jacques Maritain was at that time concerned with the reconstruction of Thomism and the rejection of some of its more sterile and dated aspects. He was professor of philosophy at the Institut Catholique in Paris from 1912 to 1933, went to the United States after the outbreak of the Second World War and returned as French ambassador to the Holy See from 1945 to 1948.

To this first generation of pioneers whose work was known to a very small circle only also belonged the two German scholars Erich Przywara and Otto Karrer. Przywara was a Jesuit priest and, in books published over a period of forty years, showed up some of the fallacies of the scholastic theological approach, preparing the ground for new theological insights and a new anthropology which encouraged others to further studies. Karrer derived his main inspiration from Newman and worked for a new ecumenical understanding of the divided Christian churches. His studies of cardinal Bellarmin, the great Catholic theologian and controversialist of the Reformation, had opened his eyes to the ecumenical issues:

I realised that the sort of theological controversy so eminently represented by Bellarmin was disastrous for the church of our time, if not perhaps for the church of the sixteenth century. My encounters with evangelical Christians taught me that they were not heretics in any real sense, that their ancestors were alienated from the Catholic church through historical events, which we are not in a position to judge, and that later generations became committed through their religious upbringing and traditional loyalties. That is why I regard as dubious and damaging any controversy conducted as it were from a distance which lacks charity and understanding.

The conflict renewed under Pius XII

The aims and ideas of these men were carried on by the next generation and it was this generation which Pius XII explicitly attacked in *Humani generis*. In Germany there were the brothers Karl and Hugo Rahner, both Jesuits, the historian of dogma, Joseph Ratzinger, the theologian Johann Metz and Hans Küng. In France there were the Jesuits Henri de Lubac and Jean Daniélou, the Dominican Yves Congar and cardinal Suhard and his supporters. Belgium produced one of the best known theologians of the Catholic renewal, the Dominican Edward Schillebeeckx. These scholars have effected the biggest revolution in theology since the baroque age, replacing, as Alfons Rosenberg put it 'the conceptual thinking of scholasticism by the vivid approach of biblical and patristic imagery'. They were responsible as theological advisers to the Council for the great turning of the tide that occurred only after the Council was launched and which ensured the influence of their ideas on the Council *schemata*. The achievements of this generation are impressively recorded, though as yet only in German, in the volumes of *Lexikon für Theologie und Kirche,* edited by Josef Höfer and Karl Rahner.

The movement found its first concrete expression in post-war France, although De Lubac, Daniélou and Congar were already known in the nineteen-thirties. It was important for De Lubac's development that in the study courses, lectures and sermons which he gave during the war, he had the opportunity of meeting communists and of coming to understand the humanist atheism advocated by them. His books on Proudhon, Feuerbach and Marx were the products of these encounters, De Lubac being one of the few Catholic theologians to take a serious interest in these modern forms of humanism. He published various books with Daniélou and Congar in the *Una Sanctum* series which Congar had started in 1937 and, with Daniélou, he edited *Sources chrétiennes,* which was a collection of patristic writings. The doctrine of grace was a favourite topic of these French theologians. De Lubac especially had contributed new insight to this doctrine, as well as to ecclesiology and pastoral sociology.

Congar's particular interest in ecumenical problems inspired his revolutionary thinking about the relations of church and world. He emphatically rejected the idea of *potestas directa* (direct power) or *potestas indirecta ecclesiae in temporalia* (indirect power of the church in temporal questions) which was still claimed by the clericalists. He was particularly concerned with the position of the laity in the church and his most famous book, *Jalons pour une*

théologie du laicat, published in 1953, was devoted to this theme. The Second Vatican Council ensured the triumph of his teachings on the church, on ecumenical relations and on the laity hardly ten years after his suspension by his superiors in 1954.

The examples of De Lubac and Congar suffice to show how the old theory of the closed and self-sufficient ghetto world of Catholicism had been as it were exploded from within. The worker-priest experiment which started in 1943 was another attempt to find a new Catholic approach to the world, but it was doomed to fail. The diffi-

A contrast of pontiffs: 239
Pius XII and Cardinal Roncalli,
later his successor John XXIII.

culties encountered by cardinal Suhard in providing pastoral care for Frenchmen conscripted to German labour camps inspired the original idea of sending priests to work in Germany as equals with their fellow countrymen. They discovered undreamt of possibilities for pastoral work. The experiment was continued after the war by some fifty priests. They hoped that the example of priests living as ordinary workers and sharing their conditions would help to win back to the church the alienated masses who had become almost completely atheist. The movement took its name from Henri Perrin's *Diary of a Worker-Priest in Germany* (1945), one of the best accounts of its origins and noble aims.

The new theology in France was the product not of a school but of the loosely-connected efforts of like-minded friends. It owed much of its vitality to the great impetus which post-war liberation had released and which also inspired the new political development of the MRP.

The beginnings of Catholic renewal in Germany were much less spectacular. The Catholic church had more or less successfully survived the Third Reich. Karl Rahner, one of the leading German Catholic thinkers, was a parish priest in a Bavarian village where he had been sent in 1944. He, his brother Hugo, Hans Urs von Balthasar (a pupil of De Lubac) and many others were active scholars, but pursued their scholarship without publicity. In spite of his outwardly somewhat cantankerous manner, Karl Rahner has nothing of the revolutionary or firebrand spirit about him. And yet his name is linked with the most astonishing upsurge of Catholic theology in modern times. His friend Johann Baptist Metz has characterised this:

Upsurge from the world of dead and rigid formulae, neo-scholastic speech and thought, resolutely confronting the scholastic tradition with the transcendental and existential questions of modern philosophy; upsurge from the separation of theology and *kerygma* (proclamation), so that a theology passionately devoted to its aims, ever questioning, most scientific in method, would in the long run also prove to be the most *kerygmatic* theology, that is, most sincerely devoted to the main Christian task of communicating the 'glad tidings'; upsurge from the faith of theological officialdom towards a fraternal faith; upsurge, finally, from the ghetto mentality of ideologies towards the dialogue in a pluralist society.

Paradoxically, Rahner's achievement is due to his sense of tradition and his – in the best sense of the word – conservative approach, which never allowed his thinking to stray from the historical paths of the church. This enabled him when he was attacked and suspected of heresy in Rome to continue at the centre of German Catholic theology, and also to influence many who would have hesitated to follow him had he been a more revolutionary leader. His great triumph, like Congar's, was that at the Council Catholicism suddenly took note of his ideas and his way of thinking.

Schillebeeckx, like Rahner and Congar, maintains a positive attitude towards the modern processes of secularisation and therefore to the world in its present form, but he has perhaps gone further than they in rejecting the neo-scholastic approach. His *Sakramentele Heilsökonomie* ('Sacramental economy of redemption'), published as his dissertation, caused something of a theological sensation and profoundly influenced Catholic thinking in Holland and Belgium. Along with Congar, Rahner, Ratzinger and Küng, he was among the most influential theological advisers to the Council.

But not even the achievement and significance of these theologians can fully explain what has come to be known as the miracle of the Second Vatican Council. Indeed, the hour had certainly come for the church to open up towards the world, and towards a speculative theology aware of the problems of humanity instead of only sectional interests. It was also to be foreseen that the church was bound to be the loser in the fight against modernism. But if the charge about the alleged modernist conspiracy was ever justified, it would apply to this group of French and German theologians.

Their personal attitude was probably one of the most important reasons for their success. Neither Congar, Rahner nor Schillebeeckx are great writers able to persuade through the elegance of their arguments. For a long time their influence did not extend beyond a limited number of theologians. And they were careful to avoid all polemics against Rome – a temptation which Tyrrell, Loisy or Schell were temperamentally incapable of resisting, and which naturally made them even more suspect. In the end, Rome was overwhelmed by the strength of their case, and the majority of the Council Fathers realised that the curial position had become untenable. The optimism of John XXIII had been justified after all.

Two pontificates in perspective

By the end of the first session of the Council, on 8 December 1962, it was clearly established that the Catholic church and the papacy would no longer try to shield Catholics from meeting the world on its own terms. For over two hundred years the popes had tried to do this from a sense of pastoral responsibility and from concern for the survival of the church, but also from ignorance of the world and from an over-estimation of the dangers that might possibly arise there for the church. Of all these attempts and systems those of Pius XI and Pius XII were certainly the most impressively consistent. Their final failure was partly due to the ideas which had emerged from the struggles of the European nations to free themselves from the oppression of regimes to which the papacy had, of its own volition and with the direst consequences, committed itself. The unique chance to renew the world in the spirit of Catholicism had not been seized in 1945 because the Catholic voice was missing from those who had suffered oppression in the war and were now clamouring for freedom. This voice should have been raised in the name of Christ and his church against racialism, the most anti-Christian system that had ever dominated Europe. But in the long list of condemnations which the popes of the nineteenth and twentieth centuries have issued, none are explicitly concerned with fascism and racialism.

Perhaps in some distant future the pontificate of Pius XII with its many beneficial developments will be judged more favourably than is the case today. But one charge which has hardly as yet been heard may then be raised against him and weigh more heavily still than his silence over the crimes of Nazism. It had become clear by 1945 that the papal attempt to save Catholics from worldly contamination had failed disastrously. In France, Italy, Holland, Belgium and Germany political movements were formed which, far from being Catholic pressure groups, sought to reconstruct their countries in co-operation with other Christian forces. At first there was a possibility of carrying out this work of reconstruction in the spirit of the papal social teaching, as the *Democrazia Cristiana* in Italy, the MRP in France and the CDU in Germany had tried to do. However, in order to succeed, these forces needed the break-through of the new theological ideas which were emerging from the war and from a new Catholic vision of the world as the arena of divine activity. Pius XII who, as is well known, was aware of the church's need for reform and who had therefore himself repeatedly contemplated calling a council, prevented this development. He could not even bring himself to back unreservedly the development of Christian parties. Instead he withdrew to a position of total absolutism, though some of his addresses suggested that he was very conscious of the need for theological change. In this perspective the encyclical *Humani generis* is witness to his failure to meet the needs of the times which he himself had recognised.

By the time Roncalli succeeded him, the original impetus of the

European Christian parties had long been slowed down, and they had turned into more or less conservative movements for the defence of middle-class interests. The road was no longer open to John XXIII to use the Christian parties in his work of reconstruction. In his great encyclical *Mater et Magistra* of 15 May 1961, which already bears the stamp of his pontificate, he therefore expressed a general affirmation of modern pluralist society, and indeed explicitly stressed the obligation of Catholics to commit themselves politically by making a free and responsible choice. He thereby anticipated the place of the laity in the church as formulated later by the Council in the spirit of Congar. This was the final repudiation of the curia's claim to control the laity in all temporal and spiritual matters. The encyclical *Pacem in terris* was published on 11 April 1963, less than two months before John's death and seems almost to have been his last will and testament. It was an even more astonishing document than *Mater et Magistra* in many respects, for it challenged the world to accept peace and co-existence. To the annoyance of some, John XXIII severed the church's intimate and all too one-sided links with the west which had first been forged under Pius XII by his universal condemnation of communism. The pope thus enabled the church to begin discussions with even the communist countries.

When, after great suffering, John XXIII died on the evening of Whit Monday, 3 June 1963, one of the most revolutionary pontificates in the history of the church was ended. Since the Age of Enlightenment when the church had first learned to face a new, critical world that no longer saw things through the eyes of the church, none of the popes had dared to do what John XXIII did: to put himself at the disposal of his age and its spirit and to make the attempt of letting the spirit of Jesus Christ 'blow where it listeth'. His venture demonstrated the possibility of the pope being a representative of Christ on earth even in a pluralist and unbelieving world.

Chronology

This table does not attempt to provide a complete historical survey of ecclesiastical and political events. It lists the main events mentioned in the text, together with a few others of relevance.

List of popes	Ecclesiastical events	Political events
Pius VI 1775-99	1782 Pius' journey to Vienna 1786 Synod of Pistoia 1794 Bull *Auctorem fidei* 1799 Pius' death in exile	1789 French Revolution 1798 Republic proclaimed in Rome
Pius VII 1800-23	1801 Concordat with France 1809 Pius in exile -14 1813 Concordat with Napoleon 1814 Order of Jesuits reinstated	1809 Napoleon annexes Papal States, arrests Pius, is excommunicated. Metternich foreign minister of Austria (establishes Austrian control in north Italy) 1814 Congress of Vienna and -15 restoration of Papal States
Leo XII 1823-9	1825 Jubilee year	1828 O'Connell elected to English Parliament
Pius VIII 1829-30		1829 Catholic Emancipation in Britain 1830 July Revolution in France, Louis-Philippe elected king. Belgium achieves independence
Gregory XVI 1831-46	1832 *Mirari vos* 1834 *Singulari nos*	1831 Insurrection in Papal States suppressed with help of Austria
Pius IX 1846-78	1848 Pius flees to Gaeta	1848 Metternich resigns as foreign minister of Austria. February Revolution in France, Louis Philippe flees the country. Unification of Italy begins:

List of popes	Ecclesiastical events	Political events
		King Charles Albert of Savoy declares war on Austria, Gioberti becomes Prime Minister of Piedmont
		1849 Rome declared a republic
	1850 Papal sovereignty restored, Pius IX returns to Rome. English hierarchy restored	
		1852 Cavour becomes Prime Minister of Piedmont
	1853 Dutch hierarchy restored	
	1854 Bull *Ineffabilis* proclaims Dogma of Immaculate Conception	
		1860 Garibaldi's 'Thousand' lands in Sicily and advances up Italy, Papal States, except for Patrimony of St Peter, annexed by Italy
		1861 Victor Emmanuel becomes king of united Italy
	1864 *Quanta cura* and Syllabus of Errors	
		1867 Garibaldi's attack on Papal States repelled near Mentana Bismarck becomes Chancellor of Germany
	1868 Declaration *Non expedit*	
	1869 First Vatican Council -70 (papal infallibility declared a dogma)	
	1870 Pius 'prisoner in the -78 Vatican'	1870 Franco-Prussian war. Rome occupied by Victor Emmanuel's troops and declared capital of Italy
		1871 Bismarck begins *Kulturkampf* Rising of the commune in Paris and its defeat, Third Republic set up in France
Leo XIII 1878-1903	1878 *Quod apostolici muneris*. Scottish hierarchy restored	

List of popes	Ecclesiastical events	Political events
		1881 Tsar Alexander II assassinated
		1882 Italy forms Triple Alliance with Germany and Austria-Hungary
	1885 *Immortale Dei*	
		1886 Bismarck abandons *Kulturkampf*
	1888 *Libertas praestantissimum*	1888 William II becomes emperor of Germany
		1889 Cardinal Manning helps settle London dock strike
	1890 *Sapientiae Christianae*	1890 *Volksverein* founded in Germany; Bismarck resigns
	1891 *Rerum novarum*	
	1895 *Non expedit* made into compulsory prohibition	
	1899 'Americanism' condemned	1899 Dreyfus affair in France -1909
	1901 *Graves de communi*	
Pius X 1903-14		1905 Law of separation of church and state in France
	1906 *Vehementer nos*	
	1907 *Pascendi dominici gregis*	
		1909 *Volksbund* founded in Austria
	1910 *Editae saepe* *Le Sillon* condemned	
		1915 Italy enters First World War against Germany
	1917 New Canon Law Code	
	1918 *Non expedit* ban lifted	
		1919 Treaty of Versailles. Weimar Constitution set up in Germany. Don Sturzo founds *Partito Popolare* in Italy
	1920 *Pacem Dei munus*	
Pius XI 1922-39		1922 Mussolini comes to power in Italy
		1924 Don Sturzo exiled to London
		1925 Von Hindenberg elected President in Germany
	1926 *Action Française* condemned	1926 *Partito Popolare* suppressed by Mussolini
	1929 Lateran treaty and concordat with Italy (Vatican City State is established)	

List of popes	Ecclesiastical events	Political events
	1930 *Casti connubi*	
	1931 *Quadragesimo anno*	1932 Dollfuss becomes
	Non abbiamo bisogno	Chancellor of
		Austria
	1933 Concordat with	1933 Hitler comes to power
	Hitler	
		1934 Dollfuss assassinated
		1935 Italy invades Abyssinia
		1936 Spanish Civil War
		-9
	1937 *Mit Brennender Sorge*	
	Divini Redemptoris	
		1938 Germany annexes Austria and
		Sudetenland
Pius XII	1939 *Summi pontificatus*	1939 Germany invades Czecho-
1939-58	Concordat with Spain	slovakia
		1940 Italy enters war against France
		and England
		1943 Italy surrenders to allies
		De Gasperi founds *Democrazia Cristiana*
		1946 Italian monarchy abolished
		Mouvement républicain populaire founded in France
		1947 De Gasperi forms first government without communist participation
		1948 *Democrazia Cristiana* obtains absolute parliamentary majority
	1950 *Munificentissimus Dei*	
	Humani generis	
John XXIII	1961 *Mater et Magistra*	
1958-63	1963 *Pacem in terris*	
	Second Vatican Council	

Notes

1 E. Dammig, *Il Movimento Giansenista a Roma nella seconda metà del Secolo XVIII*, p.372, Città del Vaticano 1945.
2 Antoni, *Il problema politico dei cattolici italiani nel XIX secolo*, 1958.
3 B.Schneider-Pierre Blet-Angelo Martini, *Die Briefe Pius XII an die deutschen Bischöfe 1939-1944*, p.241, 1966.
4 Baron von Hügel, *Selected Letters 1896–1924*, p.346, London 1927.

Bibliography

Suggestions for further reading on the general background of the period covered by this book from the reign of Pope Pius VI (1775-99), to the death of John XXIII in 1963: Pastor's *History of the Popes*, (vols. 39 and 40 in the English edition). After Pastor's death his work was continued by his collaborator J. Schmidlin in his *Papstgeschichte der neuesten Zeit*, 4 vols., Munich, 1933-9, which covers the period 1800-1939. Seppelt, F.X., *Geschichte der Päpste*, 5 vols., revised by G. Schwaiger, Munich 1954-9, (from the beginnings to the French Revolution); Seppelt, F.X. and Schwaiger, G., *Geschichte der Päpste*, Munich 1964, (from the beginnings to the present day).

Aubert, R., 'L'Eglise catholique durant la première moitié du xxe siècle', *Cahiers d'Histoire Mondiale*, vol. VII, Neuchâtel, 1963, pp. 757-83. Bremond, H., *A Literary History of Religious Thought in France*, Eng. tr., vols. 1-3, London, 1938. Bucheim, K., *Geschichte der christlichen Parteien in Deutschland* Munich, 1953. Cardinale, I., *Le Saint-Siège et la Diplomatie. Aperçu historique, juridique, et pratique de la diplomatie pontificale*, Paris, Tournai, Rome, New York, 1962. Daniel-Rops, H., *L'Eglise des Révolutions. Un Combat pour Dieu, 1870-1939*, Paris, 1963. Dansette, A., *Histoire Religieuse de la France Contemporaine sous la IIIe République*, 3 vols., 1951; Eng. tr. *Religious History of Modern France*, Herder-Nelson, London, 1961. Duroselle, J.-B., *Les Débuts du Catholicisme Social en France (1822-1870)*, Paris, 1951. Ellis, J.T., *American Catholicism*, Chicago, 1965. Fliche, A. and Martin, V., *Histoire de l'Eglise depuis les origines jusqu'à nos jours*, vols. 20-26, Paris, 1949-68. Gurian, W., *Die politischen und sozialen Ideen des französischen Katholizismus (1789-1914)*, Mönchen-Gladbach, 1929. Hales, E.E.Y., *The Catholic Church in the Modern World*, New York, 1960. Hocedez, E., *Histoire de la théologie au XIXe siècle*, 3 vols., Paris, 1947-52. Hofmann, W., *Ideengeschichte der sozialen Bewegung des 19. und 20. Jahrhunderts*, Berlin, 1962. Jemolo, A.C., *Chiesa e stato in Italia del Risorgimento ad oggi*, Turin, 1949. Joset, C., *Un siècle de l'Eglise catholique en Belgique, 1830-1930*, Paris, 1930. Lenert, P., *L'Eglise catholique en Pologne*, Paris, 1962. Moody, J.N., ed., *Church and Society*, New York, 1953, contains historical essays on Catholic social and political thought and movements between 1789 and 1950: J.N. Moody, 'The Papacy, Catholicism and Society in France'; H.Hagg, 'The Catholic Movement in Belgium'; E.Alexander, 'Church and Society in

Germany'; Z.M.Ossowski, A.Zoltowski, J.Pechazek and W.Juhasz, 'Social and Political Catholicism in Poland, Czechoslovakia and Hungary'; J.N. Moody, 'Catholic Developments in Spain and Latin America'; C.Hollis, 'Social Evolution in Modern English Catholicism'; Francis Downing, 'American Catholicism in the Socio-Economic Evolution in USA'. A number of important statements by the popes and leading Catholic personalities of the period are included by way of documentation. Schnabel, F., *Deutsche Geschichte im Neunzehnten Jahrhundert*, vol. 4, *Die Religiösen Kräfte*, Freiburg, 1951. Wiseman, Cardinal, *Recollections of the Last Four Popes*, London, 1858.

State and papacy in the Age of Enlightenment and in the F. ﾟ..ch Revolution: chapters 1 and 2

Abercrombie, N., *The Origins of Jansensim*, Oxford, 1936. Acton, H.M.M., *The Bourbons of Naples, 1734-1825*, London, 1956. Belvederi, R., *Il papato di fronte alla rivoluzione e alle consequenze del Congresso di Vienna*, Bologna, 1965. Bindel, V., *Histoire Religieuse de Napoléon*, 2 vols., 1940. Consalvi, Cardinal, *Memoirs*, first published in French translation, Paris, 1864, the Italian text, *Memorie del Cardinale Ercole Consalvi*, ed. A.Signorelli, was only published in 1950 in Rome. Dammig, E., *Il movimento giansenista a Roma nella seconda metà del sec. XVIII*, Città del Vaticano, 1945. Debidour, A., *Histoire des rapports de l'Eglise et de l'Etat en France de 1789 à 1870*, Paris, 1898. Delacroix, S., *La réorganisation de l'Eglise de France après la Révolution*, 3 vols., Paris, 1962. Gorce, P. de la, *Histoire religieuse de la Révolution Française*. 3 vols., 1926. Hales, E.E.Y. *Revolution and Papacy 1769-1846*, London 1960. Heriot, A., *The French in Italy, 1796-1799*, London, 1957. Jemolo, A.C., *Il giansenismo in Italia prima della rivoluzione*, Bari, 1928. Latreille, A., *L'Eglise catholique et la Révolution Française*, 2 vols., Paris, 1946-50, and *Napoléon et le Saint Siège, 1801-1808. L'ambassade du Cardinal Fesch à Rome*, Paris, 1935. Leflon, J., *Pie VII*, Paris, 1958. Lupé, M. de, *La Captivité de Pie VII*, Paris, 1916. Maistre, J. de, *Mémoires Politiques et Correspondance Diplomatique*, Paris, 1858, and *Considérations sur la France*, Paris, 1853, which was written in 1796. Chapter 5 of the latter is entitled 'De la révolution française considérée dans son caractère anti-religieux'. Pacca, B., *Memorie Storiche di Mgr Bartolomeo Pacca sul di lui soggiorno in Germania dall'anno 1786-1794*, Rome, 1832. Passerin d'Entrèves, E., 'La politica dei giansenisti in Italia nell'ultimo Settecento', *Quaderni di cultura e storia sociale*, 1953-54 and 'La reforma "Giansenista" della chiesa e la lotta anticuriale in Italia nella seconda metà del settecento', *Rivista storica Italiana*, 71, 1959, pp. 203-34. Préclin, E., *Les Jansénistes du XVIIIe Siècle et la Constitution*

Civile du Clergé, Paris, 1929. Salvatorelli, L., *Chiesa e stato dalla rivoluzione francese ad oggi*, Florence, 1955. Vaussard, M., *Jansénisme et gallicanisme aux origines religieuses du Risorgimento*, Paris, 1959.

The origins of Christian Democracy: chapter 3

Bayle, F., *Les idées politiques de Joseph de Maistre*, Paris, 1945. Biton, L., *La contribution de la démocratie chrétienne dans la politique française*, Paris, 1954. Blaize, A., *Oeuvres inédites de F.Lamennais*, 2 vols., Paris, 1866. Boutard, C., *Lamennais: sa vie et ses doctrines*, 3 vols., Paris, 1905-13. Demarco, D., *Il tramonto dello stato pontificio. Il papato de Gregorio XVI*, Turin, 1949. Devre, J.R., *Lamennais, ses amis et le mouvement des idées à l'Epoque romantique 1824-34*, Paris, 1962. Fogarty, M.P., *Christian Democracy in Western Europe (1820-1953)*, London, 1957. Gambaro, A., *Sulle orme del Lamennais in Italia*, Turin, 1958. Geissberger, W., *Philippe-Joseph-Benjamin Buchez, Theoretiker einer christlichen Sozialökonomie und Pionier der Produktiv-Genossenschaften*, Winterthur, 1956. Gibson, The Hon. W., *The Abbé Lamennais and the Liberal Catholic Movement in France*, London, 1896. Haag, H., *Les Origines du Catholicisme libéral en Belgique 1789-1839*, Louvain, 1950. Havard de la Montagne, R., *Histoire de la Democratie chrétienne de Lamennais à Georges Bidault*, Paris, 1948. Jürgenssen, K., *Lamennais und die Gestaltung des belgischen Staates. Der liberale Katholizismus in der Verfassungsbewegung des 19. Jahrhunderts*, Wiesbaden, 1963. Lallemand, P. de, *Montalembert et ses amis dans le romantisme 1830-40*, Paris, 1927. *Articles de l'Avenir* 7 vols., Paris, 1830-2, with articles by Lamennais, Montalembert, and other liberal Catholics on political events in Europe, especially in relation to the Church. Lamennais, F., *Oeuvres complètes*, 12 vols., 1836-7, and *Tradition de l'Eglise sur l'Institution des Evêques*, 3 vols., 1818, and *Essai sur l'Indifférence en matière de religion*, 4 vols., (Eng, tr. Lord Stanley of Alderley, 1895), and *Affaires de Rome*, Paris, 1836. The early editions also include the Latin and French texts of the encyclical *Mirari vos*. Lecannuet, Le P.E., *Montalembert*, 3 vols., Paris, 1895-1902. Leslie, R.F., *Polish Politics and the Revolution of November 1830*, Athlone Press, 1956. Maier, H., *Revolution und Kirche. Studien zur Frühgeschichte der christlichen Demokratie (1798-1901)*, Freiburg-Breisgau, 1965. Mollat, G., *La question romaine de Pie VI à Pie XI*, Paris, 1932. Morelli, E., *La politica estera di T.Bernetti, Secretario di Gregorio XVI*, Rome 1957. Moulinié, H., *De Bonald*, Paris, 1915. Rohden, P.R., *Joseph de Maistre als politischer Theoretiker*, Munich, 1929. Rovan, J., *L'Histoire de la démocratie chrétienne*, 2 vols., Paris, 1956. Spaemann, R., *Der Ursprung der Soziologie aus dem Geist der Restauration. Studien über L.G.A. de Bonald*, Munich, 1959.

Vaussard, M., *Histoire de la democratie chrétienne* (in France, Belgium, Italy), Paris, 1956. Vidler, A. R., *Prophecy and Papacy. A Study of Lamennais, the Church and the Revolution*, London, 1954. Ward, B., *The Eve of Catholic Emancipation*, 2 vols., London, 1911.

Pio Nono and the fall of the Papal States : chapter 4

Antoni, E., *Il problema politico dei cattolici italiani hel XIX secolo* Rass. stor. it. 4, 1958. Aubert, R., *Le Pontificat de Pie IX 1846-1878*, Paris, 1952. Cameron, R.E., 'Papal Finance and the Temporal Power, 1815-71', *Church History*, No. 26 New York, 1957. Fernesolle, O., *Pio IX Papo*, vol. 1, *1792-1855*, Paris, 1960. Hales, E.E.Y., *Pio Nono. A study in European politics and religion in the nineteenth century*, London, 1954. Mollat, G., *La question romaine de Pie VI à Pie XI*, Paris, 1932. Petrocchi, M., *La restaurazione romana 1815-43*, Florence, 1943. Rosmini, A., *Della Missione a Roma*, Turin, 1881. Serafini, A., *Pio Nono*, vol. 1, *1792-1846*. Vercesi, E., *I Papi del secolo XIX*, vol. 1, *Pio VII, Napoleone e la restaurazione*, Turin, 1933; vol. 2, *Tre pontificati: Leone XII, Pio VIII, Gregorio XVI*.

The victory of neo-scholasticism and the Vatican Council : chapter 5

Acton, Lord, *Essays on Church and State*, ed. Douglas Woodruff, London, 1952. (containing Acton's important essays on 'Ultramontanism', 'The States of the Church', 'The Political System of the Popes' and 'The Munich Congress 1863'), and *Essays on Freedom and Power*, ed. Gertrude Himmelfarb, Boston, 1948, (containing Acton's essays on 'Conflicts with Rome' and 'The Vatican Council'). Altholz, J.L., *The Liberal Catholic Movement in England. The 'Rambler' and its contributors 1848-1864*, London, 1962. Butler, C., *The First Vatican Council*, London, 1925. Conzemius, V., ed. *Briefwechsel Ignaz von Döllinger – Lord Acton*, vol. 1: *1850-1869*, vol. 2: *1869-70*, Munich, 1963-5. Foucher, Abbé L., *La philosophie catholique en France au XIX siècle avant la renaissance thomiste et dans son rapport avec elle*, Paris, 1955. Friedrich, J., *Ignaz v. Döllinger*, 3 vols., Munich, 1899-1901. Gasquet, F.A., ed., *Lord Acton and his Circle*, London, 1906. Himmelfarb, G., *Lord Acton, a study in conscience and politics*, London, 1952. Leetham, C., *Rosmini – Priest, Philosopher and Patriot*, London, 1957. Lenhart, L., *Bischof Ketteler, Staatspolitiker – Sozialpolitiker – Kirchenpolitiker*, 3 vols., Mainz, 1966-8. MacDougall, H.A., *The Acton-Newman relations. The dilemma of Christian Liberalism*, New York, 1962. Mathew, D., *Lord Acton and his Times*, London, 1968, and *Catholicism in England*, London, 1955. Panichi, V., *La Civiltà Cattolica e la politica ecclesiastica italiana durante il pontificato di Leone XIII.* Schiel, H., *Franz Xavier Kraus und die katholische Tübinger Schule*, Ellwangen, 1958. Ward, W., *Life of John Henry Cardinal Newman*, 2 vols., London, 1912.

Modernism and integrism: chapter 8

Bedoyère, M. de la, *The Life of Baron von Hügel*, London, 1951. Congar, Y., 'Mentalité de droite et intégrisme', *La Vie intellectuelle*, Paris, June, 1950. De Rosa, G., *Storia del movimento cattolico in Italia*, I: *Dalla restaurazione all'età giolittiana*, II: *Il partito popolare italiano*. Heiler, F., *Alfred Loisy*, Munich, 1957. Hoog, G., *Histoire du Catholicisme Social en France, 1871-1931*, Paris, 1946. Larkin, M.J., 'The Vatican, French Catholics and the "associations culturelles"', *The Journal of Modern History*, No. 36, 1964, pp. 298-317. Loisy, A., *Memoires pour servir à l'histoire religieuse de mon temps*, 3 vols., 1930-1. Marlé R., ed. *Au coeur de la crise moderniste. Le dossier inédit d'une controverse. Lettres de M.Blondel, H.Brémond, Fr.v.Hügel, A. Loisy*, Paris, 1960. Pezet, E., *Chrétiens au service de la cité, de Léon au Sillon et au M.R.P. Idées, militants, réalisations de la democratie chretienne en France de 1891 à 1965.* Poulat, E., *Histoire, dogme et critique dans la crise moderniste*, Paris, 1962. Rollet, H., *L'Action sociale des catholiques en France, 1871-1901*, 1947. Sedgwick, A., *The Ralliement in French politics, 1890-1898*, Cambridge, Mass., 1965.

Church and state under Leo XIII, Pius X and Benedict XV: chapter 9

Antonazzi, G., ed. *L'enciclica Rerum Novarum*, Rome, 1957. Barbier, E., *Histoire du Catholicisme Libéral et du Catholicisme Social en France, du Concile du Vatican à l'avènement de S.S. Benoit, 1870-1914*, 6 vols., Bordeaux. 1924. Crispolti, F., and Aureli, G., *La politica di Leone XIII da l.Galimberti a M.Rampolla*, Rome, 1912. Hayward, F., *Un pape méconnu, Benoit XV*, Paris, 1955 and *Le dernier Siècle de la Rome Pontificale*, 2 vols., 1928. Lecanuet, Le P.E., *La Vie de l'Eglise sous Léon XIII. L'église de France sous la Troisième République*, Paris, 1930. McAvoy, T.T., *The Great Crisis in American Catholic History 1895-1900*, Chicago, 1957. Migliori, G., *Benedetto XV*, Milan, 1955. Mitchell, H., *Pie X et la France*, Paris, 1954, and *Le Cardinal R.Merry del Val, Secrétaire d'Etat de Saint Pie X*, Paris, 1956. Monetti, G., *Leone XIII*, 3 vols., Rome, 1942. Soderni, E., *Il pontificato di Leone XIII*, 3 vols., Milan, 1932-3. Thomas, L., *L'Action Française devant l'Eglise de Pie X à Pie XII*, Paris, 1965. Tischleder, P., *Die Staatslehre Leos XIII*, Mönchen-Gladbach, 1925. Vercesi, E., *Tre Papi – Leo XIII, Pio X, Benedetto XV*, Milan, 1929, and *Il pontificato de Pio X*, Milan, 1935.

The Concordats: chapter 11

Albrecht, A., *Koordination von Staat und Kirche in der Demokratie*. (A juridical investigation of the legal problems arising in the concordats between the Catholic church and western democratic governments), Freiburg-Breisgau, 1965. Aretin, K.O.von., 'Prälat Kaas, Franz von Papen und das Reichskonkordat von 1933', *Vierteljahrshefte für Zeitgeschichte*, No. 14, 1966, pp. 252-79.

Catholic Action: chapter 12

Dalla Torre, G., *Azone Cattolica e fascismo. Il conflitto del 1931*, Rome, 1945. Falconi, C., *Gedda e l'Azione Cattolica*, Parenti, 1958.

Relations between Italy and the Vatican 1922-63: chapter 13

Bergen, W. von., *Der Einfluss der Lateranverträge auf die staatliche Gesetzgebung Italiens*, Düsseldorf, 1954. Binchy, D.A., *Church and State in Fascist Italy*, London, 1941. Canaletti Gaudenti, A., *Luigi Sturzo. Il pensiero e le opere*, Rome, 1945. De Rossi, G.dell-Arno, *Pio XI e Mussolini*, Rome, 1954. Kerdreux, M. de, *Pie XI. Dans l'intimité d'un grand pape*, Mulhouse, 1963. Petrocchi, G., *Don Luigi Sturzo*, Rome, 1945. Sturzo, L., *Church and State*, Eng. tr., London, 1939.

The papacy 1918-63: chapter 14

Altmeyer, K.A., *Katholische Presse unter N.S. Diktatur*, Berlin, 1962. Blet, P., Martini, A., Schneider, B., Graham, R., edd. *Actes et documents du Saint Siège relatifs à la seconde guerre mondiale*, vol. 1: *Le Saint Siège et la guerre en Europe, Mars 1939-Août 1940*, Città del Vaticano 1965; vol. 2: *Letters de Pie XII aux Evêques allemands, 1939-1944*, Città del Vaticano, 1966. Dansette, A., *Destin du Catholicisme Français, 1926-1956*, Paris, 1957. Deuerlein, E., *Der Deutsche Katholizismus 1933*, Osnabrück, 1963. Einaude, M., and Goguel, F., *Christian Democracy in Italy and France*, University of Notre Dame Press, Ind., 1952. Esposito, R.F., *Processo al Vicario. Pio XII e gli ebrei secondo la testimonianza della storia*, Turin, 1965. Favara, E., *De iure naturali in doctrina Pii Papae XII*, Rome, 1966. Friedlander, S., *Pius XII and the Third Reich*, London, 1966. Giovannetti, A., *Il vaticano e la guerra 1939-40*, Città del Vaticano, 1960. Harrigan, W.M., 'Nazi Germany and the Holy See: The Historical Background of *Mit brennender Sorge*', *Catholic Historical Review*, No. 47, 1961-2. Hochhuth, R., *The Representative*, London,

1963. Lewy, G., *The Catholic Church and Nazi Germany*, New York, 1964. Mammarella, G., *Italy after fascism. A political history 1943-1965*, University of Notre Dame Press, Ind., 1966. Montero, A., *La persecución religiosa en España 1936-39*, Madrid, 1962. Regatillo, E.F., *El Concordato español de 1953*, Santander, 1961. Tardini, Cardinal, *Pie XII*, Paris, 1961. Tracy, G.M., *Découverte de Pie XII. Ce qu'on n'a jamais dit*, Paris-Geneva, 1966. Weinzierl, E., ed. *Kirche in Österreich 1918-1965*, 2 vols., Vienna-Munich, 1966-7. Wilson, J.F., *Church and State in American history*, London, 1966.

Towards the Vatican Council: chapter 15

Aradi, Z., with Michael Derrick and Douglas Woodruff: *John XXIII, Pope of the Council*, London, 1961. Bea, Cardinal, *The Unity of Christians*, London, 1963. Bosworth, W., *Catholicism and Crisis in Modern France,* Princeton, 1962. Calvez, J.-Y., *Eglise et Societé Economique*, vol. 1, *L'enseignement social des papes de Léon XIII à Pie XII*, Paris, 1959; vol. 2, *L'enseignement social de Jean XXIII*, Paris, 1963. Carillo de Albornoz, A.F., *Le Catholicisme et la liberté religieuse*, Paris, 1961. Fogliasso, E., *Papa Giovanni spiega come giunse alla Pacem in terris*, Rome, 1964. Guitton, J., *L'Eglise et les laïcs de Newman à Paul VI*, Paris, 1963. Gurian, W., and Fitzsimons, M.A., *The Catholic Church in World Affairs*, University of Notre Dame Press, Ind., 1954, an account of the Catholic church shortly before the Second Vatican Council, with contributions on Church-State relations by John Courtney Murry, SJ; on Democracy and the Church by Oskar Bauhofer and Yves R.Simon; Catholicism in Germany by Otto B.Roegele, in France by Adrien Dansette, in Italy by M.F.Sciacca, in Spain by Rafael Calvo Serer and in England by M.A.Fitzsimons; the Catholic Church in the United States by Thomas McAvoy and Aaron I. Abell; the Church in Latin America by Peter Masten Dunne, SJ. Jemolo, A.C., *Chiesa e Stato in Italia negli ultimi cento anni*. The 1963 edition brings the survey down to the time of John XXIII. John XXIII, *The Diary of a Soul*, London, 1965. Kaiser, R., *Inside the Council*, London, 1963. Kerdreux, M. de, *Le pape de la bonté, Jean XXIII*, Mulhouse, 1966. Küng, H., *The Council and Reunion*, London, 1961. Lazzarini, A., *John XXIII*, London, 1960. Purdy, W.A., *The Church on the move. The characters and policies of Pius XII and John XXIII*, New York, 1967. Runne, X., *Letters from Vatican City*, London, 1963. Schultz, H.J., ed., *Tendenzen der Theologie im 20. Jahrhundert. Eine Geschichte in Porträts*, Stuttgart-Olten, 1967. Webster, R., *Christian Democracy in Italy 1860-1960*, London, 1961. Wenger, A., *Vatican II, Première Session*, Editions du Centurion, 1963.

254

Index

256